INTERNATIONAL DEVELOPMENT IN FOCUS

Artisanal Small-Scale Gold Mining

A Framework for Collecting Site-Specific Sampling and Survey Data to Support Health-Impact Analyses

KATHERINE VON STACKELBERG, PAMELA R. D. WILLIAMS, AND ERNESTO SÁNCHEZ-TRIANA

 **WORLD BANK GROUP**

Contents

Boxes

Figures

Tables

Acknowledgments

This report was prepared by a team that included Katherine von Stackelberg, Pamela R. D. Williams, Santiago Enriquez, Claudia Serrano, and Ernesto Sánchez-Triana (Task Team Leader). The extended task team included Gabriela Elizondo, Montserrat Meiro-Lorenzo, Mayra Guerra Lopez, Maria Rosa Puech, and Kalterine Vrenezi. This report was edited by Stan Wanat (Stanford University).

Valuable guidance was provided by peer reviewers Shafick Hoossein (Environmental Specialist), Maged Mahmoud (Lead Environmental Specialist, Environment, Natural Resources and Blue Economy Global Practice in Africa), and Frank Van Woerden (Lead Environmental Engineer, Environment, Natural Resources and Blue Economy Global Practice in the Middle East and North Africa).

This analytical work was supervised by Karin Kemper (Global Director, Environment, Natural Resources and Blue Economy Global Practice—ENB), and Iain Shuker and Christian Peter (Practice Managers, Global Platform Unit, ENB). This analytical work was funded by the Pollution Management and Environmental Health Multi-Donor Trust Fund (PMEH).

Overview

Artisanal small-scale gold mining occurs informally and therefore relies on low technologies and extraction methods lacking pollution controls. As a result, despite the fact that artisanal small-scale gold mining produces only 20 percent of the world's gold, it releases more mercury than any other sector[1] and represents the largest source of mercury emissions at nearly 38 percent (UNEP 2018).[2] In Africa alone, it is estimated that gold production from large- and small-scale artisanal mining is responsible for nearly 45 percent of mercury emissions.[3]

At various points during the gold mining process, mercury is released and emitted into the atmosphere, where it deposits into soil, lakes, and rivers. According to the United Nations Environmental Programme (UNEP), artisanal small-scale gold mining releases more than 700 tons of mercury into the atmosphere and 800 tons of mercury onto land and into water each year (UNEP 2013).[4] The World Health Organization (WHO) considers mercury one of the top 10 chemicals leading to major public health concerns.[5] The human health effects of mercury are varied but typically include impacts to the nervous, digestive, and immune systems. Mercury contamination is particularly worrisome for young children and pregnant women, causing both physical and mental disabilities. Of the 19 million people employed in artisanal small-scale gold mining (Steckling et al. 2017),[6] as many as 5 million are women and children (UNEP). Safety for workers has also become a particular concern given the poor working conditions in countries where safety measures are lacking, resulting in frequent occupational incidents.[7]

In the last few years, mercury use and production have declined in the United States. While mercury can still be found in such places as Alaska, California, Nevada, and Texas, mercury has not been mined as a principal mineral since 1992 in the US. According to the United States Geological Survey (USGS), only two mercury cell plants operated in the United States in 2019. Additionally, in 2008, the Mercury Export Ban was introduced, and in 2013, the ban on the export of elemental mercury from the United States was implemented. Nonetheless, while mercury use and production have decreased in the United States, its use is still prevalent around the world. In 2019, global mine production was estimated at approximately 4,000 metric tons, with China alone responsible for 3,500 metric tons. Similarly, out of the 600,000 tons of mercury resources in the world, countries like China, Kyrgyzstan, and Peru are considered to have the largest reserves[8].

Protecting communities, workers, and the environment from the toxic chemicals in artisanal small-scale gold mining requires legalizing and formalizing the industry to establish effective regulatory responses. The Minamata Convention on Mercury is a global treaty to protect human health and the environment from the adverse effects of mercury[9]. Agreed upon and adopted in 2013, the convention entered into force in 2017. The Minamata Convention seeks to control the releases of mercury throughout its lifecycle. Actions have included bans on new mercury mines and the phaseout of existing ones, the phaseout of mercury use in several products and processes, control measures on emissions and releases, regulation of the informal sector of artisanal and small-scale gold mining, and the storage and disposal of mercury. While the Minamata Convention has a global reach, with more than 124 ratifications, there still is a need for additional regulations in more localized communities.

In 2019, the *State of Artisanal and Small-Scale Mining Report* identified key data gaps that need to be addressed to formalize the global artisanal small-scale gold mining sector. These gaps include a lack of a standardized research methodology for evaluating sites and shared data repositories. One of the challenges to developing effective environmental regulation is lack of evidence linking contaminants from specific mining sites to adverse health outcomes in individuals. Although information on toxic exposure is available, such information has traditionally been collected for high-income countries and may not be reliable or accurate for assessing exposures in low- and middle-income countries.

This report aims to address some of these research gaps by providing a standardized methodology to assess the relationship between environmental contamination, exposure, biomonitoring, and health outcomes related to contaminants originating from artisanal small-scale gold mining, including mercury, methylmercury, lead, and arsenic. The guidelines also standardize the collection of environmental and biological samples and seek to build local capacity to conduct environmental assessments. Based on a consistent sampling and data-collection methodology, data can be seamlessly linked across sites, contaminants, and geographic areas. Through these assessments, potential community impacts can be assessed, leading to potential regulations to limit future exposures, protecting surrounding populations from toxic sites. A rigorous process must be followed to successfully, and appropriately, evaluate the impact that ASGM sites have on exposed populations, particularly on vulnerable individuals. The process consists of a set of sampling programs through which researchers collect information and data at the household level to compare between individuals within the exposed population and individuals within an unexposed/reference population. These guidelines provide recommendations for each step of the process. Likewise, information on the different contaminants in ASGM sites is presented, including important details such as their exposure pathways, possible health effects, and tools used to collect and measure their concentrations across different media. This report also addresses potential challenges facing researchers, and alternatives or solutions to these challenges.

This framework document provides a pragmatic approach for designing representative studies and developing uniform sampling guidelines to support estimates of morbidity that are explicitly linked to exposure to land-based contaminants from artisanal small-scale gold mining activities. A primary goal is to support environmental burden of disease evaluations, which attempt to attribute health outcomes to specific sources of pollution. The guidelines provide recommendations on the most appropriate and cost-effective sampling and analysis methods to ensure the collection of representative population-level data, sample-size recommendations for each contaminant and environmental media, biological sampling data, household-survey data, and health-outcome data.

STRUCTURE OF THE REPORT

Chapter 1 of the guidelines provides an overview of the ASGM process, including a description of the primary contaminants released or discharged during each step of the process. This chapter also presents a general conceptual site model (CSM) for ASGM sites that identifies the transport mechanisms, exposure pathways, and routes of exposure for local populations who may be exposed to these contaminants. Lastly, this chapter highlights key site-specific questions or issues that should be considered to inform the selection of participating households and sampling locations at ASGM and reference sites.

Subsequent chapters of the guidelines provide guidance for information gathering and data collection during field implementation at ASGM sites. Chapter 2 describes the process for identifying participating households and individuals within those households that will provide household survey data (appendix B), environmental sampling data (chapter 3), biomonitoring data (chapter 4), and health-outcomes data (chapter 5). Identifying participating households is a critical step that will determine where to conduct subsequent environmental sampling of soil, sediment, dust, water, fish, or agricultural and food products, and will be the focus of biological and health-outcome data for assessing the potential contribution of ASGM-related contamination to population-level exposures and health outcomes in exposed individuals. Chapter 3 provides general guidelines for conducting environmental sampling of soil, dust, sediment, water, fish, or agricultural and food products. Chapter 4 provides general guidelines for collecting biomonitoring samples in blood, urine, hair, or other biological matrices. Chapter 5 provides general guidelines for evaluating health outcomes using medical exams, health surveys, and diagnostic tests.

NOTES

1. US EPA (US Environmental Protection Agency). 2012. *Reducing Mercury Pollution from Artisanal and Small-Scale Gold Mining.* Washington, DC: US EPA. http://www.epa.gov/oia/toxics/mercury/asgm.html
2. https://wedocs.unep.org/bitstream/handle/20.500.11822/27579/GMA2018.pdf?sequence=1&isAllowed=y
3. Dabrowski et al. 2008. "Anthropogenic Mercury Emissions in South Africa: Coal Combustion in Power Plants." *Atmos Environ* 42: 6620–26.
4. http://wedocs.unep.org/bitstream/handle/20.500.11822/7984/-Global%20Mercury%20Assessment-201367.pdf?sequence=3&isAllowed=y
5. https://www.who.int/ipcs/assessment/public_health/chemicals_phc/en/
6. https://www.sciencedirect.com/science/article/pii/S2214999616308207
7. Weiss et al. 2016. *Chemical Pollution in Low- and Middle-Income Countries.* https://www.eawag.ch/fileadmin/Domain1/Abteilungen/sandec/publikationen/Chemical_Pollution/Lamics-WEB.pdf

8. USGS (US Geological Survey). 2020. Mineral Commodity Summaries (January). https://pubs.usgs.gov/periodicals/mcs2020/mcs2020-mercury.pdf

9. Minamata Convention on Mercury. *Text and Appendixes.* http://www.mercuryconvention.org/Convention/Text/tabid/3426/language/en-US/Default.aspx

Abbreviations

AAS	atomic absorption spectrophotometry
As	arsenic
ASGM	artisanal small-scale gold mining
ATSDR	US Agency for Toxic Substances and Disease Registry
BMI	body mass index
CBC	complete blood count
Cd	cadmium
CDC	US Centers for Disease Control and Prevention
CIMI	chronic inorganic mercury intoxication
CoC	contaminant of concern
COPD	chronic obstructive pulmonary disease
CRP	C-reactive protein
CSM	conceptual site model
CVAAS	cold vapor atomic absorption spectrometry
CVD	cardiovascular disease
ECD	early childhood development
ECDI	Early Childhood Development Instrument
EPA	US Environmental Protection Agency
FDA	US Food and Drug Administration
FEF	forced expiratory flow
FEV	forced expiratory volume
FVC	forced vital capacity
Hg	mercury
HICs	high-income countries
ICP-MS	inductively coupled plasma–mass spectrometry
IEUBK	biokinetic model for lead in children
IOMC	Inter-Organization Programme for the Sound Management of Chemicals
IPCS	International Programme on Chemical Safety
ISO	International Organization for Standardization
LMICs	low- and middle-income countries
MeHg	methylmercury
MELQO	Measuring Early Learning Quality and Outcomes (UN)

NIH	US National Institutes of Health
Pb	lead
PBPK	physiologically based pharmacokinetic models
PFT	pulmonary-function testing
PMEH	Pollution Management and Environmental Health
RBP	retinol-binding protein
UNEP	United Nations Environment Programme
US EPA	United States Environmental Protection Agency
USGS	United States Geological Survey
WHI	Women's Health Initiative
WHO	World Health Organization
XRF	X-ray fluorescence

1 Overview of the Artisanal Small-Scale Gold Mining Process

INTRODUCTION

This chapter provides an overview of the artisanal small-scale gold mining (ASGM) process, including a description of the primary contaminants released or discharged during each step of the process. This chapter also presents a general conceptual site model (CSM) for ASGM sites that identifies the transport mechanisms, exposure pathways, and routes of exposure for local populations who may be exposed to these contaminants.

Problem formulation is the process of establishing study objectives, supporting the identification of data-quality objectives associated with statistical analyses, and developing a strategy for characterizing the zone of influence or community footprint associated with ASGM activities in a specific geographic area. A detailed checklist is provided to assist in developing a land-use map of the area and to refine the general CSM for the site of interest based on site-specific existing information and knowledge. The provided checklists highlight key site-specific questions or issues required to inform the selection of participating households and sampling locations at ASGM and reference sites.

DESCRIPTION OF THE ASGM PROCESS

Informal small-scale ASGM activities are occurring in many low- and middle-income countries (LMICs). Figure 1.1 provides an overview of the steps involved during typical ASGM operations:

- Extraction: During ore extraction, alluvial deposits (river sediments) or hard-rock deposits are identified, sediment or overburden is removed, and the ore is mined by surface excavation, which can include pumping sediments from river bottoms and related activities.
- Processing: In this step, the gold is separated from the ore. Processing methods vary depending upon the type of ore. Gold particles in alluvial deposits are often already separated and require little mechanical treatment. Crushing and milling are required for hard-rock deposits. Primary crushing can be

FIGURE 1.1

Steps in typical artisanal small-scale gold mining (ASGM) operations

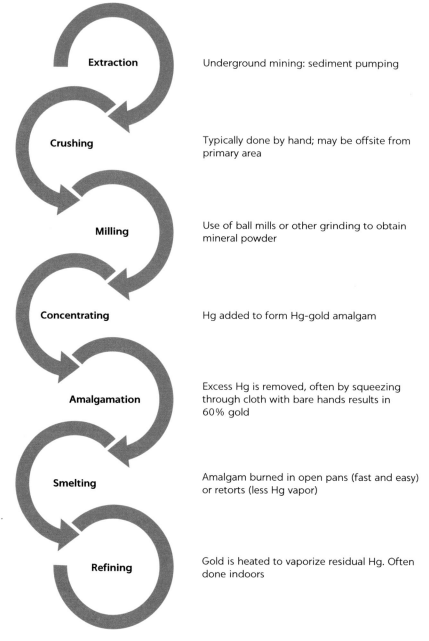

Extraction — Underground mining: sediment pumping

Crushing — Typically done by hand; may be offsite from primary area

Milling — Use of ball mills or other grinding to obtain mineral powder

Concentrating — Hg added to form Hg-gold amalgam

Amalgamation — Excess Hg is removed, often by squeezing through cloth with bare hands results in 60% gold

Smelting — Amalgam burned in open pans (fast and easy) or retorts (less Hg vapor)

Refining — Gold is heated to vaporize residual Hg. Often done indoors

Source: Based on Kristensen, Thomsen, and Mikkelsen 2014.
Note: Hg = mercury.

done manually—for example, using hammers—or with machines. Mills are then used to grind the ore into smaller particles and ultimately to a fine powder.

• Concentrating: Depending on the specific process, gold may be further separated from other materials using wet or dry processes. Different methods and technologies (for example, sluices, centrifuges, vibrating tables) exist to concentrate the extracted gold. Gold density is higher as compared with other minerals in the ore. Therefore, many techniques utilize gravity-based approaches in water.

- Amalgamation: Elemental mercury is used to obtain an equal parts mercury-gold alloy referred to as amalgam. The two main methods used in ASGM for amalgamation are whole-ore and concentrate amalgamation. In whole-ore amalgamation, large quantities of elemental mercury (Hg) are added to the alloy, and most of the Hg is released as waste into the mine tailings due to the inefficiency of this process. In concentrate amalgamation, Hg is added only to the concentrated alloy (step above), resulting in considerably less Hg being used and allowing the excess Hg to be recovered. The amalgam is then heated in various stages to release the mercury, with increasing levels of purity of the gold.
- Smelting: The amalgam is heated, which vaporizes the mercury and separates the gold. In "open burning" smelting operations, all of the Hg vapor is emitted to the air. The gold produced by amalgam burning is porous and referred to as "sponge gold."
- Refining: Sponge gold is further heated to remove residual Hg and other impurities.

Mercury, both elemental (Hg) and the organic form methylmercury (MeHg), is the primary contaminant of concern (CoC) at ASGM sites, followed by Pb (from lead ore if used), and to a lesser extent, arsenic (As). It is important to recognize that the specific process used in the extraction of gold, as well as the composition of the ore materials (for example, lead ores), will be unique to each ASGM location and will dictate the specific contaminants that are generated. Hg enters the environment during various phases of the mining process, as do Pb and As, depending on the source materials. Table 1.1 describes expected discharges from ASGM activities and the environmental fate of these discharges. Appendix A provides a brief overview of the metals typically found at ASGM sites.

Once released or discharged into the environment, the contaminants from ASGM sites can migrate through different environmental media based on their chemical and physical properties and local conditions. Hg is also readily converted to MeHg in aquatic environments, where it can bioaccumulate in sediment and fish species. The primary transport mechanisms at ASGM sites include the following:

- Airborne transport of fugitive dust from contaminated surface soil
- Airborne transport of vapors and particulate downwind from the source
- Leaching or runoff of contaminated soil to surface water or groundwater (particularly following rain or flooding events)
- Leaching of waste products from lagoons or pits to surface water or groundwater sources

TABLE 1.1 **Contaminant discharges from ASGM activities**

OUTPUTS	MECHANISM
Hg vapor and particulate	Released to air and soil during the entire process
Pb particulate	Released to air and soil during processing
Mine tailings containing Hg, Pb, and As	Discharged to unlined lagoons or pits
Wastewater containing Hg, Pb, and As	Discharged to soil or surface water

Source: World Bank.
Note: As = arsenic; Hg = mercury; Pb = lead.

- Migration of contaminated surface water from wastewater discharges to other surface water sources or groundwater
- Migration of contaminated surface water from wastewater discharges to other surface water sources or groundwater
- Conversion of Hg to MeHg in aquatic environments and bioaccumulation in sediment and fish species.

CONCEPTUAL SITE MODEL FOR ASGM SITES

Once contaminants have migrated offsite at ASGM sites, additional processes or activities can lead to population exposures to these contaminants through direct or indirect contact with contaminated environmental media. This is described in figure 1.2.

For example, vaporized (elemental) Hg is released during the burning process and emitted into the atmosphere, where it oxidizes and is deposited into soil, lakes, rivers, and oceans via both wet and dry deposition. As mentioned above, bacteria can also transform Hg into the organic form, MeHg, which readily accumulates in aquatic food webs (for example, fish and shellfish), potentially leading to significant exposures in individuals who consume fish and shellfish.

As the mined ores are mechanically ground and processed, significant amounts of Pb dust are released into the air, and this process may occur in residential areas outside the primary mining area as individuals bring chunks of ore home. Dry milling, which is commonly employed during the processing stage, tends to magnify the level of dust produced, and in many areas, processing may occur within housing areas using the same mortars and pestles used to prepare food. Even when this processing occurs outside of residential areas, miners often return home with clothes contaminated with Pb. Additionally, there is evidence that children may travel to the mines to sell food and will therefore be exposed directly to Pb dust and Hg vapor near the mining sites, and possibly facilitate

FIGURE 1.2

General conceptual model of potential exposures at ASGM sites

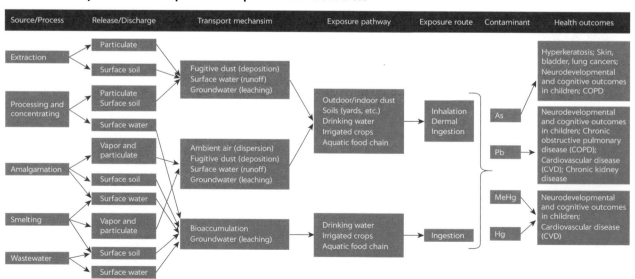

Source: von Stackelberg, Williams, and Sánchez-Triana 2021.
Note: As = arsenic; Hg = mercury; MeHg = methylmercury; Pb = lead.

indirect exposures by bringing unsold (cross-contaminated) food back into residential areas. In addition to airborne transport of Pb dust, the grinding and sluicing process often occurs near water sources, which can result in contamination of surface water with Pb and initiate the Hg–MeHg conversion process.

An *exposure pathway* refers to the physical movement of an agent from a source or point of release through the environment to a receptor (for example, air, groundwater, surface water, soil, sediment, dust, food chain). *Exposure routes* describe the different ways by which agents may enter the body following external contact (for example, inhalation, ingestion, dermal). Potential exposure pathways and routes of exposure related to ASGM sites are presented in table 1.2, and a generic site conceptual model is presented in figure 1.2.

TABLE 1.2 **Potential exposure pathways by exposure route and environmental media originating from ASGM sites**

EXPOSURE ROUTE	ENVIRONMENTAL MEDIA		
	AIR	SOIL AND DUST	WATER
Inhalation	Inhalation of Hg vapors and Hg, Pb, or As particles in outdoor air due to releases to air during entire process or during crushing and milling of ore	Inhalation of Hg soil vapors and Hg, Pb, or As particles or dust in outdoor air due to releases to soil during entire process or during crushing and milling of ore or from mine tailing or wastewater discharges to water	Inhalation of Hg or Pb vapors released from tap, surface, or groundwater (for example, bathing, showering, washing, swimming) due to mine tailing or wastewater discharges to water
	Inhalation of Hg vapors and Hg, Pb, or As particles in indoor air due to releases to air during entire process or during crushing and milling of ore	Inhalation of Hg soil vapors and Hg, Pb, or As particles or dust in indoor air due to releases to soil during entire process or during crushing and milling of ore or from mine tailing or wastewater discharges to water	
Ingestion	Ingestion of agricultural products contaminated with Hg, Pb, or As due to deposition of vapors or particles (for example, fruits, vegetables, grains)	Incidental ingestion of Hg, Pb, or As in soil or dust (indoors or outdoors) due to releases to soil during entire process or during crushing and milling of ore and from mine tailing or wastewater discharges to soil	Ingestion of Hg, Pb, or As in tap, surface, or groundwater due to mine tailing or wastewater discharges to water
	Ingestion of agricultural products contaminated with Hg, Pb, or As due to transfer of contaminants from air to animals or plants to animals (for example, meat, milk, eggs)	Ingestion of agricultural products contaminated with Hg, Pb, or As by transfer of contaminants from soil to plants, animals, or plants to animals	Ingestion of Hg, Pb, or As in agricultural products due to being irrigated with contaminated water
			Ingestion of Hg, Pb, or As in agricultural products due to transfer of contaminants from water to animals
			Ingestion of MeHg in fish/shellfish due to deposition of Hg and methylation to MeHg in sediments
Dermal contact	Dermal contact with Hg vapors and Hg, Pb, or As particles due to releases to air during entire process or during crushing and milling of ore	Dermal contact with Hg, Pb, or As in soil or dust (indoors or outdoors) due to releases to soil during entire process or during crushing and milling of ore and from mine tailing or wastewater discharges to soil	Dermal contact with Hg, Pb, or As in tap, surface, or groundwater due to mine tailing or wastewater discharges to water

Source: World Bank.
Note: As = arsenic; Hg = mercury; MeHg = methylmercury; Pb = lead.

LINKING ENVIRONMENTAL CONTAMINATION TO HUMAN EXPOSURES AND HEALTH OUTCOMES

Exposure is the amount of chemical in the environmental media that a person comes into contact with and is a function of the exposure point concentration and the amount of time the individual is in contact with the contaminated media. *Intake* is the amount of chemical that enters the human body via an exposure route. Characterizing exposure and intake therefore requires information about various *exposure factors* such as behavior, time and activity patterns, and contact rates. Common exposure factors relevant for ASGM sites include the following:

- Soil and dust ingestion rates
- Water and liquid ingestion rates
- Food and fish/shellfish ingestion rates
- Inhalation rates
- Mouthing frequency in children (hand-to-mouth and object-to-mouth)
- Dermal exposure factors (for example, skin surface area, skin adherence, residue transfer)
- Time spent indoors versus outdoors
- Time spent in various activities (for example, sleeping, at school, at work)
- Time spent bathing, showering, or swimming
- Time spent playing on various surfaces (for example, dirt, grass, sand, gravel)
- Body weight.

Although information on typical or recommended exposure factors is available from the literature, this information has traditionally been collected for high-income countries (HICs) and may not be reliable or accurate for assessing exposures in LMICs. Site- and population-specific information should be collected to provide relevant exposure factors data for use at ASGM sites. (Appendix B provides links to key resources for designing and conducting home surveys.) This information will be linked to the environmental sampling data (described in chapter 3) as one way to estimate population-level exposures in areas where ASGM activities occur.

Dose is the amount of chemical that crosses the outer boundary of an organism and is absorbed into the body and available for interaction with metabolic processes. The internal dose of a chemical (or its metabolite) can be measured directly from biological sampling (often called biomonitoring). Depending on the contaminant, common biological matrices that may be relevant for ASGM sites include the following:

- Blood
- Urine
- Hair
- Nails (that is, toenails and fingernails)
- Breast milk or cord blood.

As discussed further in chapter 4, "General Guidelines for Biological Sampling," samples should be collected from relevant biological matrices, where feasible, at each ASGM site to provide data on total exposures from all sources and pathways (as reflected by the measured internal dose). This information will be linked to the household survey data (chapter 2) and exposure concentration (chapter 3) to assess the relationship between estimates of exposure and biomarkers of exposure. Appendix D provides links to key resources and methods for collecting biological samples. Where possible, these data will also be used to validate or update existing modeling tools (appendix D) for estimating population exposures and doses. Note that prior to collecting any biological samples, the in-field team will need to ensure that all Institutional Review Board (IRB), human subject, and ethical clearances are completed as required.

Population exposures to predominant metals at ASGM sites may be associated with different types of health outcomes, as shown in table 1.3 and described in chapter 4.

As discussed in chapter 5, "General Guidelines for Health-Outcomes Assessment," medical exams, surveys, and diagnostic testing should be conducted, where feasible and appropriate, at each ASGM site to provide data on reported, observed, or measured symptoms and health effects. This information will be linked to the household survey (chapter 2), environmental concentrations (chapter 3), and biological dose measurements (chapter 4) to assess the potential relationship between exposures and health outcomes at ASGM sites. Appendix E provides links to key tools and resources for assessing health outcomes.

Figure 1.3 provides an overview of how the data collected at each ASGM site will be used to link environmental contamination to human exposures and health outcomes.

PROBLEM FORMULATION AND SITE-SPECIFIC CHARACTERIZATION

The primary objective of these guidelines is to guide research to assess the relationship between environmental contamination, exposures, and health outcomes related to a subset of contaminants originating from ASGM activities (for example, Hg, MeHg, Pb, and As) for particularly vulnerable populations (for

TABLE 1.3 **Health outcomes associated with contaminants of concern at ASGM sites**

METAL	MEASURABLE HEALTH OUTCOMES
Hg	Developmental and cognitive deficits in children
	Neurotoxicity (for example, tremors, ataxia) in children and adults
	Renal health outcomes in children and adults
MeHg	Developmental and cognitive deficits in children
Pb	Developmental and cognitive deficits in children
	Cardiovascular health outcomes in adults
	Renal health outcomes in children and adults
As	Skin rashes and lesions and hyperkeratosis, possible precursors to skin cancer
	Developmental and cognitive deficits in children
	Lung cancer in adults
	Bladder cancer in adults

Source: World Bank.
Note: As = arsenic; Hg = mercury; MeHg = methylmercury; Pb = lead.

FIGURE 1.3

Overview of how site data will be used to link environmental contamination to human exposures and health outcomes

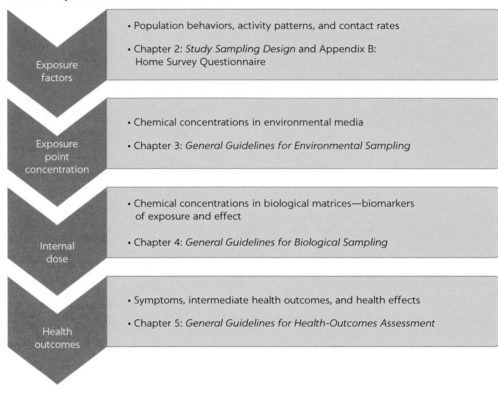

Source: World Bank.

example, children, women of child-bearing age) within a single household at ASGM sites in LMICs. To achieve this objective, biomonitoring and health-outcome data are linked to household survey and environmental data (for example, soil, dust, water, fish, or agricultural products) for individuals within an "exposed" population compared to individuals within an "unexposed" or reference population. Data on exposures and health outcomes in the same individual across a representative set of individuals is required to support an understanding of the potential impacts of ASGM activities on local communities. Statistical analysis of the data obtained through this research will answer questions such as the following:

- What are the environmental concentrations of Hg, MeHg, Pb, and As in the vicinity of ASGM activities? Are environmental concentrations higher in areas with direct exposures as compared to areas without such activities?
- What are the biological concentrations of Hg, MeHg, Pb, and As in blood, hair, or urine in exposed populations? Do these levels correlate with environmental concentrations? Do these levels differ between ASGM-exposed populations and non-ASGM-exposed populations?
- What is the incidence of specific health outcomes in ASGM-exposed populations? Do observed health outcomes correlate with environmental or biological concentrations? Do health outcomes differ as compared to non-ASGM-exposed populations?

- How do time-activity patterns and exposure factors differ across populations? Can observed time-activity patterns help explain the biological or health-outcome findings at ASGM sites?
- Which data sets are most predictive of exposures or health outcomes? Is there a reduced set of data that can be collected in the future to streamline the evaluation of potential impacts from ASGM activities?
- Can an assessment framework be developed to evaluate the benefits and costs of potential interventions to reduce exposures or improve population health at ASGM sites?

Problem formulation is the process of establishing study objectives, supporting the identification of data-quality objectives associated with statistical analyses, and developing a strategy for characterizing the zone of influence or community footprint associated with ASGM activities in a specific geographic area. A key first step is to develop a land-use map of the area and refine the general CSM for the site of interest based on site-specific existing information and knowledge. This will set the stage for subsequent collection of environmental, household survey, biomonitoring, and health-outcomes data given the primary objective described above.

A goal of problem formulation is to assemble existing site information and data to inform an understanding of how small-scale ASGM activities might affect the local population in a general sense, which is then used to develop a site map of the broader study area ("site map"). The map may be developed using local topographical maps, Google Maps, Google Earth, geographic information system (GIS) programs, or similar software.

The map should include a defined geographic area (for example, village, town, city) that locates all ASGM activities and processing areas (that is, "source areas") relative to other infrastructure or areas where populations, particularly children, spend the most time (for example, housing units, schools, town center, and so forth), since these define the potential zone of influence or footprint associated with ASGM activities. For the purposes of this manual, these areas are collectively referred to as the "ASGM study site" and include both the source area as well as the broader zone of influence.

Note that it is not uncommon for individuals to take chunks of ore from the primary ASGM processing area to their homes for extraction and processing. Additional maps or insets provide the spatial context for activities that may lead to contaminant exposures. For example, within various source areas, the map should identify where specific ASGM activities occur and the disposition of waste products, such as where mine tailings are stored, where processing activities occur, and where wastewaters are discharged from various processing activities.

The map should also identify the prevailing wind direction and the location of local wells or water bodies (particularly those used as drinking water sources or for recreational purposes) as well as direct and indirect wastewater discharges (including proximity to freshwater and sources of drinking water). The site map should also specify the locations where fishing may occur, since releases of Hg and subsequent methylation to MeHg and bioaccumulation in aquatic environments can represent a significant exposure pathway for local anglers. The site map will also serve as the basis for identifying households from which environmental sampling will occur (chapter 3) as well providing home survey data (appendix B), biomonitoring data (chapter 4), and health-outcome data (chapter 5).

Another goal of problem formulation is to refine the general CSM for ASGM sites to reflect any unique characteristics of the study area and identify the relevant site-specific exposure pathways and exposed populations of interest. Thus, problem formulation is used to characterize all aspects of the environmental setting and determine where and under what conditions general population exposures are likeliest to occur. The following checklist is designed as a guide to assist in characterizing and mapping the environmental setting and establishing the zone of influence to develop the site-specific CSM.

CSM Checklist

Characterize the general environmental setting on one or more maps:

- Locate ASGM activities in the context of local populations, noting where different aspects of the process may occur. In some areas, grinding and milling occur in local homes.
- Identify locations of all surface waters, including ditches, creeks, streams, rivers, and lakes.
- Identify what is known about groundwater, depth to the water table, and aquifers in the study area.
- Identify the prevailing wind direction, particularly relative to residential areas, local water bodies, and small- or large-scale agricultural activities.
- Identify water bodies within a depositional area of ASGM activities or affected by wastewaters or soil runoff. Microbial transformation of mercury to methylmercury and subsequent uptake into aquatic organisms may be an important exposure pathway.
- Identify agricultural areas, community gardens, and the potential for backyard gardening.
- Locate sources of irrigation water that might be affected by ASGM discharges, including direct or indirect surface-water discharges or releases to soils that can run off or erode. Establish whether groundwater is used for irrigation and whether there is a leaching pathway.
- Identify locations where animals or animal products (for example, milk, eggs) are raised for consumption.

Describe the ASGM process:

- Identify the source of ores used in the process—lead and arsenic are of concern at ASGM sites.
- Calculate the approximate volume (average monthly or annual) of gold production.
- Describe the specific ASGM process utilized and identify all inputs and outputs (for example, see figure 1.1).
- Identify the specific amalgamation process (for example, whole ore or concentrated).
- Establish the disposition of mining tailings and note where they are stored/kept. A key concern with ASGM activities is the biotransformation of mercury to methylmercury, particularly in aquatic environments.
- Establish where process waters are discharged. A key concern with ASGM activities is the biotransformation of mercury to methylmercury, particularly in aquatic environments.

Waste releases and potential fate and transport:

- Develop a qualitative mass balance for ASGM activities by identifying all materials used in the process, where they come from, and what products, including waste, are generated.
- Locate wastewater discharges on the site map and identify the specific hydrologic connections between wastewater discharges and surface waters (for example, ditches, lagoons, receiving waters).
- Establish whether typical precipitation events lead to routine ponding and discharges to nearby surface waters with the potential for bioaccumulation into aquatic organisms.
- Locate communal surface or groundwater sources of drinking water relative to potentially impacted surface waters on the site map to identify potential sampling areas.
- Establish the potential for wastewater discharges (directly or indirectly through surface water) to be used as irrigation water for local agricultural products or animals.
- In some areas, ASGM processes such as grinding and milling occur in disparate locations, including homes and other public areas removed from areas where amalgamation occurs. These locations need to be identified and waste disposition documented. For example, what happens to the dust generated through these activities?

Population demographics and exposure pathways:

- Establish the local population and population size (for example, village, urban, peri-urban).
- Quantify or estimate population size and age/sex distribution.
- Identify the fraction of the local population that participates in ASGM activities.
- Identify residential areas relative to ASGM activities on the site map.
- Identify and map community spaces within the study area, including schools, hospitals and health centers, community centers, places of worship, playgrounds, and places where individuals, particularly children, are likely to spend significant amounts of time.
- If processing activities occur in homes (for example, grinding and milling), these specific locations should be explicitly identified.
- Establish site-specific exposure pathways (as shown in figure 1.2).
- Identify whether unique or additional exposure pathways should be considered. Particular emphasis should be given to identifying the sources of drinking water and whether fish consumption occurs, either through recreational angling or commercial operations with fish/seafood going to local markets.

The following chapters provide recommendations for specific data-collection efforts at each ASGM site, starting with the identification of sampling households that provide the linkage between environmental exposures and community health outcomes. These guidelines provide a general (uniform) approach for data collection across the relevant domains (for example, environmental samples, biomonitoring, exposure factors, and health outcomes); however, detailed field protocols (for example, the physical process of collecting samples, storing and shipping samples, laboratory analysis of samples) and sampling data sheets will need to be provided by the in-field research team, recognizing that local analytical capacity to implement these guidelines will differ across countries.

Local implementation may involve an iterative process in which initially split samples are collected and sent for analysis locally as well as to an accredited international laboratory for a standard interlaboratory comparison. Enhancing and leveraging local capacity to conduct sampling, analyze samples, and interpret results is expected to require flexibility and collaboration.

Specific statistical analyses will depend on the number of participating households (chapter 2) and the specific numbers of samples collected for each domain. These guidelines are directed toward the overall goal of relating community CoC exposures associated with land-based contamination from ASGM sites to health outcomes and that data (for example, environmental exposure, human behavior, biomonitoring, and health outcomes) collected across these different domains will be combined to explore the burden of disease associated with ASGM activities. Within each domain and across domains, many different statistical and modeling approaches are available to explore possible correlations and associations (for example, different kinds of regression models, odds ratios, relative risks, logistic models, and statistical versus mechanistic models). There is a greater likelihood of being able to combine data and the results of studies conducted at different times and places with varying objectives if the studies follow consistent data-collection methods. Consequently, the goal of these guidelines is to ensure optimal data collection to better inform decision-making more broadly.

REFERENCES

Kristensen, A. K. B., J. F. Thomsen, and S. Mikkelsen. 2014. "A Review of Mercury Exposure among Artisanal Small-Scale Gold Miners in Developing Countries." *International Archives of Occupational and Environmental Health* 87 (6): 579–90. doi:10.1007/s00420-013-0902-9.

von Stackelberg, K., P. R. D. Williams, and E. Sánchez-Triana. 2021. "A Systematic Framework for Collecting Site-Specific Sampling and Survey Data to Support Analyses of Health Impacts from Land-Based Pollution in Low- and Middle-Income Countries." *International Journal of Environmental Research and Public Health* 18 (9): 4676. doi:10.3390/ijerph18094676.

2 Study Sampling Design

INTRODUCTION

This chapter describes the process for identifying participating households and individuals within those households that will provide household survey data (appendix B), environmental sampling data (chapter 3), biomonitoring data (chapter 4), and health-outcomes data (chapter 5). Identifying participating households is a critical step that will determine where to conduct subsequent environmental sampling of soil, sediment, dust, water, fish, or agricultural and food products, and will be the focus of biological and health-outcome data for assessing the potential contribution of artisanal small-scale gold mining (ASGM)-related contamination to population-level exposures and health outcomes in exposed individuals.

To meet the primary research objective, the sampling design is structured to link environmental contamination and individual exposures to multiple contaminants of concern (CoCs) with different health outcomes associated with exposure to these CoCs at the household level. Selected households and sampling locations should therefore provide data on how environmental contamination contributes to household exposures, rather than identifying local hot spots or fully characterizing environmental concentrations across the entire site, which will likely require a different sampling strategy. These guidelines recommend a primary grid-based sampling design strategy augmented by targeted sampling where individuals spend significant amounts of time (for example, schools, playgrounds, agricultural locations, fish from recreational or commercial fishing areas). Targeted sampling will be required for households associated with fish consumption from potentially affected aquatic areas. Typical grid densities range from 20m x 20m to 100m x 100m, with most falling generally in the 40m x 40m to 60m x 60m range. A household is selected from each grid node with an example provided.

Recommendations for the home survey questionnaire are designed to provide the detailed information on exposure factors such as time-activity patterns, food-frequency questionnaires, and other demographic information used to link environmental sampling data with biomonitoring data and health-outcome data in a specific community. As these data are collected, they should be compiled into country- or region-specific databases to support development of risk assessments and other analyses that require quantifying exposure factors (for example, consumption rates, body weight, and so forth) to predict, for example, contaminant-specific intake rates applicable to analyses beyond ASGM sites. Of particular interest will be fish-consumption patterns, quantities, and choices of species.

As noted in chapter 1, the primary CoCs at ASGM sites include mercury (Hg), methylmercury (MeHg), and lead (Pb), and to a lesser extent, arsenic (As), depending on the source of ores used. These metals will generally persist in the environment in their original form. MeHg and Hg are likely to be measured in fish and water and perhaps some agricultural products, soil, and dust, while Pb and As will be measurable in soil, dust, water, and agricultural products, with lesser amounts in fish (As in seafood is converted to a largely nontoxic organic form of As and is less relevant for As exposures). Determining where to collect environmental samples (that is, households and targeted locations) at each ASGM site should be informed by knowledge of the source location, contaminant-release and transport mechanisms, likely exposure pathways, and location and activities of populations exposed, per the refined conceptual site model (CSM) discussed in chapter 1 and household survey described below and in appendix B.

IDENTIFYING PARTICIPATING HOUSEHOLDS AND SAMPLING LOCATIONS

The first critical step prior to any in-field data collection efforts is to identify the households and other targeted sampling locations where individuals spend time in the vicinity of each ASGM site. Assuming the primary study objective is to understand how localized exposures associated with ASGM activities are associated with community health outcomes, a reference location will also need to be selected that is environmentally similar but without the contaminated site.

In these guidelines, a combination of grid-based and targeted sampling is recommended for identifying participating households. With respect to grid-based sampling at ASGM sites, households are identified using regularly spaced intervals defined by a grid placed over the study area or discrete areas within the study area, which helps ensure randomization in the selection process. By contrast, targeted sampling at ASGM sites will be identified by the in-field research team on an as-needed basis to account for potential exposures arising at a certain location or among a specific subpopulation, such as consumers of locally caught fish.

Consequently, the in-field research team will need to carefully identify processing areas and methods as discussed in chapter 1 in order to identify households and obtain samples from areas in which anticipated exposures are highest, which will differ between Hg or MeHg and Pb. Specifically, the source of Hg is primarily vapor, which is emitted into the air and can be transported over greater distances (for example, several km), versus Pb, which is emitted primarily as dust and is typically deposited within one km of processing activities. There is also the potential for processing activities to occur in different locations if workers bring ores home, which may lead to broader population exposures in distinct housing areas removed from the primary processing area.

Additionally, airborne Hg may be deposited on local water bodies and undergo methylation and subsequent uptake into aquatic food webs. Households that consume fish from these water bodies are likely to experience MeHg exposures originating from ASGM activities. Therefore, ensuring that some, if not all, of the households selected to provide biomonitoring and health-outcome data actually consume fish from one or more impacted water bodies will be important if this is identified as a potential exposure pathway; otherwise, there will be no clear linkage between exposure, biomonitoring, and health outcomes. This may necessitate some informal survey research at potentially impacted water bodies to identify fish consumers for targeted sampling who may be highly exposed.

Within each selected household, children ages 10 years and younger represent a vulnerable population of interest at ASGM sites, given that all the CoCs are associated with neurodevelopmental outcomes in children. Children also have a greater opportunity for Hg, MeHg, and Pb exposures at these sites due to activity patterns and on a per body weight basis, and tools are available for evaluating specific health outcomes (for example, cognitive deficits) associated with elevated childhood exposures to these metals. Adult populations are also of interest at ASGM sites, particularly women of childbearing age. Fish-consumption advisories exist in many parts of the world due to the possibility of MeHg exposures from contaminated fish. Therefore, the preferred hierarchy of populations to target at ASGM sites is as follows: (a) male and female children ages 3 to 10 years old, (b) women of childbearing age, and (c) men and women of any age.

Although a more refined approach for selecting households at each site can be tailored by the in-field research team once the specific ASGM sites have been identified, the following steps will assist in identifying households and environmental sampling locations at these sites using a consistent and uniform approach.

Step 1

Based on the initial site characterization process and site map developed in chapter 1, overlay an equally spaced grid (typically a square or rectangle but can be a circle or other shape) on the site map with the source area at the center, assuming the source area is surrounded by residential areas. Depending on the site, the source area may not be centered within a residential area and the grid will need to be adjusted accordingly to capture locations designed to maximize potential exposures.

As noted above, it may be appropriate to identify distinct sampling areas within the larger study area if, for example, ASGM activities occur on the outskirts of a city and it is known that (a) individuals bring ores home for processing and these homes are located within distinct housing communities, and (b) there are one or more known water bodies known to be affected by ASGM activities. The goal is to identify households within the zone of influence of the source area as informed by the refined CSM (chapter 1), recognizing that the zone of influence is likely to differ between Hg or MeHg and Pb.

Determining the exact grid size (which affects the sample size) will require some flexibility, depending on the site-specific CSM, population density, and resource constraints. Typical grid densities range from 20m x 20m to 100m x 100m, with most falling generally in the 40m x 40m to 60m x 60m range. A household is selected from each grid node. If a selected household is not willing to participate in the study, a neighboring household in the same grid space should be chosen. The sample size can be altered by choice of grid size—that is, reducing the grid size will increase the number of sample nodes and households sampled, while increasing the grid size will reduce the number of sample nodes and households sampled. Although it is not possible to identify a predetermined sample size for each site using power calculations, to balance research objectives and feasibility constraints, it is recommended that more than 100 households, but fewer than 400 households, be selected per ASGM site (average of 200 to 300 households).[1] See appendix B for additional references.

For this ASGM example, households and targeted sampling locations are selected as follows: First, to identify households, a square 50m x 50m grid is imposed over the entire area. However, because portions of the study area are uninhabited and without households, these grid nodes are subsequently removed from the total grid nodes, and only those grid nodes in residential areas are sampled. A 50m x 50m grid = 2,500m^2 overlaid on a study area of 1,800m x 1,600m = 2.88 km^2 results in 1,152 individual grid nodes. Once the grid nodes corresponding to uninhabited areas are removed, 230 individual grid nodes (corresponding to 230 households) remain. Second, targeted sampling is used to select the four homes where localized milling and grinding occur. Additionally, at least 15 children frequent the primary processing area to sell food, and the parents of all 15 are approached as potential participants in the study, of which 10 households agree. Moreover, as noted, this ASGM site contains an affected water body and consumption of recreationally caught fish is identified as a potential exposure pathway. Because there is no guarantee that households selected via the grid-based sampling will contain any fish consumers, additional targeting of anglers at an identified water body will be conducted using an informal survey over several days to identify 20 additional households for inclusion in the study. Therefore, in total, 230 grid-based households, 4 households at which auxiliary processing occurs, 10 households at which children are known to frequent the primary processing area, and 20 fish-consuming households are selected for inclusion in the study (that is, a total of 264 households).

Step 2

In addition to identifying households using the grid-based sampling approach described in Step 1, targeted sampling may be necessary to capture the potential range of exposures in the population based on population-specific characteristics.

As mentioned, at ASGM sites it is not uncommon for (a) individuals to bring ores home for processing, and (b) consumption of locally caught fish from one or more affected water bodies. Therefore, households should be selected from areas where home-based ore processing occurs using a separate grid or in a targeted way based on information obtained through initial site visits. Similarly, for fish consumption, if it is primarily recreationally caught fish, then an informal survey (see example) or local knowledge should be used to target specific households for sampling that are known to consume fish. Alternatively, if fish are sent to a central market, it may make sense to select random individuals purchasing fish to ensure this exposure pathway is represented in the study design.

Finally, targeted sampling will likely be required at locations where study participants spend significant amounts of time, notably schools and other community areas. Identifying the final list of targeted locations may require input from the household survey responses.

Step 3

For all households identified in Steps 1 and 2, select two household members to participate in the study. All subsequent environmental, biological, and health-outcome sampling will link back to the specific characteristics and activity patterns of these individuals, which will be informed by the home survey responses. As noted above, the primary population of interest for this study is children ages 10 or younger, and one child and that child's mother should be selected for participation. However, some households may not contain children within this age grouping or provide permission for a young child to participate in the study. In these situations, an older child under the age of 18 and that child's mother should be selected, if possible; otherwise, seek permission for any adult in the household.

Given the objective to link the home survey, biomonitoring, and health-outcome data to environmental exposures, the home survey should be conducted as soon as the households and participating individuals have been identified. Information gathered from the survey will provide important data on additional targeted sampling locations if these have not already been identified (for example, water bodies and associated fish, schools, playgrounds, and communal drinking-water sources). Appendix B provides sample questions and additional information on designing household questionnaires. A particularly useful reference with respect to ASGM sites is guidance developed by the United Nations Environment Programme and the World Health Organization, specifically designed to identify populations potentially at risk from Hg and MeHg exposures (UNEP and WHO 2008).

The home survey questionnaire (summarized in table 2.1 and described more fully in appendix B) provides detailed information on exposure factors such as time-activity patterns, food frequency questionnaires, and other demographic information used to link environmental sampling data (chapter 3) with biomonitoring data (chapter 4) and health-outcome data (chapter 5) in a specific community. However, as these kinds of data are collected, this information should be compiled into country- or region-specific databases to support development of risk assessments and other analyses that require quantifying exposure factors (for example, consumption rates, body weight, and so forth) to predict, for example, contaminant-specific intake rates. Standardized tables of exposure factors (for example, the US Environmental Protection Agency's "Exposure Factors Handbook: 2011 Edition" [EPA 2011]) have been derived for specific countries, but it is not clear how these data represent communities from areas with different cultural and lifestyle attributes.

In general, each participating individual (or a parent on behalf of a child) will answer the types of questions shown in table 2.1.

Step 4

For each ASGM site, identify a matched reference site that has similar features and population characteristics that does not participate in ASGM activities but is expected to experience similar environmental exposures in the absence of ASGM activities and conduct sampling at this site in the same manner as the ASGM site. This step is recommended given the objective to determine the association between site-related contamination and health outcomes in the general population. The statistical comparison between two populations similar in every

TABLE 2.1 **Categories of questions in the home survey (appendix B)**

CATEGORY	TYPE OF QUESTIONS
General demographics	Age, sex, length of residence, education, income, household size, and composition
Occupation and school	Work and school activities, possibility for take-home/outside-of-the-home exposures
Time-activity patterns and lifestyle	Exposure factors and lifestyle/housing details, including other possible sources of exposure
Dietary information	Calculate intake rates based on a food frequency questionnaire (FFQ), with an emphasis on information about consumption of locally produced agricultural products (either home garden or purchased). FFQs can be done by keeping a diary over some time period or recall over some time period (for example, 24-hour recall). Can be combined with a duplicate diet analysis. In addition, note drinking-water sources (communal untreated, municipal treated) and amount of water and water-based beverage consumption
Economic data	Cost-of-illness
Health status	Self-reported symptoms—may be superseded by an on-site or off-site medical examination in conjunction with biomonitoring (chapter 4) and health-outcome evaluation and testing (chapter 5)

Source: World Bank.

way except for the exposure of interest (for example, no ASGM activities of any kind in the reference population) will provide important insights into site-related contamination. Although it is possible to evaluate associations without a reference population, the results may not be as definitive.

Note that achieving an objective other than the primary objective identified here might require a different sampling approach or different sample-size requirements. For example, a more complete characterization of environmental CoC concentrations throughout a study area without also collecting biomonitoring and health-outcome data might require additional environmental sampling (for example, soil, dust, water) than is recommended in chapter 3, which targets individual households and other locations where individuals spend the most time in order to link environmental exposures most efficiently and effectively with biomonitoring and health-outcome data. Similarly, a study focused on characterizing population exposures to CoCs based on biomonitoring data (chapter 4) in the absence of environmental data may require a larger grid over a larger area to ensure a representative sample of the general population.

NOTE

1. Because the current study design is focused on multiple CoCs and exploratory associations between multiple endpoints (for example, environmental contamination, individual exposures, several possible health outcomes per CoC), it is not possible to conduct a single statistical power calculation to determine optimal sample size at ASGM sites. A useful reference is a WHO publication by Lwanga and Lemeshow (1991), which provides tables of minimum numbers of samples given specific hypotheses and inputs. In general, power calculations involving contaminant exposures and health outcomes will depend on the statistical approach(es) to be used in analyzing the data, anticipated effect sizes, and/or the difference between two populations and will be based on (a) anticipated probability of a health outcome given no exposure (general prevalence in the population), (b) anticipated relative risk, (c) confidence level, (d) significance level, and (e) relative precision.

REFERENCES

Lwanga, S. K., and S. Lemeshow. 1991. *Sample Size Determination in Health Studies: A Practical Manual.* Geneva: World Health Organization.

UNEP and WHO (United Nations Environment Programme and World Health Organization). 2008. "Guidance for Identifying Populations at Risk from Mercury Exposure." Report for the Inter-Organization Programme for the Sound Management of Chemicals (IOMC) issued by the UNEP DTIE Chemicals Branch and WHO Department of Food Safety, Zoonoses and Foodborne Diseases, Geneva.

US EPA (United States Environmental Protection Agency). "Exposure Factors Handbook: 2011 Edition." Report, National Center for Environmental Assessment, Office of Research and Development, EPA, Washington, DC.

3 General Guidelines For Environmental Sampling

INTRODUCTION

This chapter provides an overview of environmental media that may be affected by artisanal small-scale gold mining (ASGM) activities, as well as specific recommendations for sampling strategies at each household and sampling area. This chapter also makes recommendations for appropriate analytical methodologies, and provides a running example for identifying sampling locations, and for collecting and analyzing samples from each participating household and targeted sampling area.

Environmental samples will be used to determine the overall magnitude of contamination at each ASGM site, with an emphasis on those where populations of interest spend the most time. This chapter provides general guidelines for sample collection at each sampling location (sampling design) and what types of samples should be collected from different environmental media. Important factors that will need to be considered on a site-by-site basis are also noted. Detailed protocols and procedures for collecting a physical sample, handling and preparing a physical sample, and laboratory analysis of physical samples are not addressed here and will be developed by the in-field research team based on existing guidance, as summarized in appendix C. It is essential that the environmental sampling be conducted for the same homes and individuals for whom the home survey (appendix B), biomonitoring (chapter 4), and health-outcome (chapter 5) data are collected. The same type of environmental samples should also be collected from both the identified ASGM sites and matched reference sites. Note that any necessary ethical clearances will need to be obtained prior to sample collection by the in-field research team.

The in-field research team should provide detailed protocols and procedures for collecting a physical sample, for handling and preparing physical samples, and for laboratory analysis of physical samples. Field observation and data sheets should also be provided by the in-field research team. It is important that all sampling tools and containers be clean and free of contaminants prior to sampling.

SOIL SAMPLING

Exposure pathways and routes

The primary contaminant of concern (CoC) released or discharged at ASGM sites into the environment is mercury (Hg), which transforms to methylmercury (MeHg) in aquatic environments (as well as interstitial spaces in soil), lead (Pb), and arsenic (As). Because these metals do not degrade easily in the environment, they are likely to be found in both surface and subsurface soils at ASGM sites. Populations in contact with soils at ASGM sites, particularly surface soil, include both adults and children, although the latter are more likely to have direct and more frequent contact with surface soil because of their behaviors and activity patterns.

Dermal contact and incidental, direct, and indirect ingestion of contaminated surface soils may be important routes and pathways of exposure at ASGM sites. Dermal exposures can occur when adults or children walk barefoot on surface soil or their body touches this soil (for example, during play outdoors, or specific activities such as children spending time in mining or processing areas). Incidental ingestion can occur when individuals get soil on their skin (for example, fingers) or an object (for example, a toy), which then comes into contact with their mouth or food. Direct ingestion can occur when individuals eat dirt or soil (this is a common practice among some children and generally still involves the top layer of soil), whereas indirect ingestion can occur when crops are grown in contaminated soil (for example, below-ground root vegetables) or are affected by fugitive dust or airborne soils (for example, above-ground leafy vegetables).

Sampling protocol and analysis

Soil samples should be collected at each ASGM and reference site using the grid sampling approach described in the previous chapter. Specifically, soil samples should be collected near the ASGM source area, in off-site processing areas, and in areas (for example, yards and gardens) corresponding to selected households. Additional targeted soil samples should be collected at schools or daycare facilities (for example, playgrounds) or from any other outdoor area where participating household members spend significant amounts of time (for example, outdoor recreational areas).

It is important that specific sampling locations within each household or targeted location be optimized relative to where individuals spend the most time (for example, child playing in yard versus near the front door, child playing in playground at school versus parking lot). Note that sample locations should preferably consist of bare soil that is not covered with grass, vegetation, or other material. Because individuals are more likely to come into contact with surface soils than subsurface soils, only surface-soil sampling is recommended at ASGM sites.

When collecting soil samples, the following general guidelines should be used (see example in box 3.1):

- Identify four individual undisturbed (or minimally disturbed) soil-sampling locations per household or sampling location. The four locations should be

> **Important Note**
> Soil sampling should occur in the same households or locations where other environmental samples are being collected and that relate to individuals providing biomonitoring and health-outcome data.

Box 3.1

Soil-sampling strategy at a hypothetical ASGM site

A total of 254 individual soil samples will be taken from 230 individual households, 4 auxiliary processing households, and 20 households with known fish consumers. At the 10 households with children who sell food at the mining area, the home survey revealed they spend most of their time at the primary mining area; thus, sampling will preferentially be conducted there, but if resources allow, home sampling should also occur (table B3.1.1). In addition, the household survey (appendix B) revealed that many children attend one of the three schools in the area, and these are additionally targeted, for a total of 258 sampling locations (for the 10 children who frequent the mining area, only one sample is required to capture those exposures). Each composite sample consists of four individual samples, which are analyzed for Hg, Pb, and As in the field using an XRF analyzer (the composite samples are packaged and sent to an accredited laboratory for analysis of Hg, Pb, and As at a minimum). In addition, one out of four (25 percent) of the samples (rounded up to 63) taken from the 250 individual households (230 plus the 20 fish-consuming households) will be analyzed for Pb bioavailability, as well as the 3 elementary schools, 4 auxiliary processing households, and the mining area, for a total of 71 samples.

Soil sampling at homes or schools includes those areas where individuals spend the most time (for example, front or back yard, garden, playground, and processing). The emphasis is on those individuals for whom the home survey, biological sampling, and health-outcome data will be collected, and these individuals also represent the focal point for all environmental sampling.

TABLE B3.1.1 **Examples of three households selected for sampling**

HOUSEHOLD	INDIVIDUAL	TIME ACTIVITY	SAMPLING LOCATIONS
1	8-year-old child (m)	This is a household where a parent brings home ore for off-site processing and the child plays nearby.	Four individual samples (XRF) from around the area where the child plays and processing occurs; composited for the lab.
2	10-year-old child (f)	Mother spends most of her day selling food at the mining site.	Four individual samples (XRF) from the area where selling occurs; composited for the lab—note this location will apply to the other nine children known to sell food as well.
3	28-year-old mother (f)	Mother takes care of her young children in a communal area in a housing complex.	Four individual samples (XRF) from the communal area; composited for the lab.

Source: World Bank.
Note: XRF = X-ray fluorescence.

representative of the entire area(s) where the population of interest spends the most time and over which activities occur. This could involve collecting the four samples from different spots within the same location (for example, front yard or garden) or from different spots at multiple locations (for example, front yard and back yard).

- Record all four sampling locations using Global Positioning System (GPS) and document coordinates on the site map.
- Collect the surface-soil samples at a depth of 0 cm to 10 cm. (Note: the zero level starts from the surface after removal of any vegetation, fresh litter, and surficial stones.)

- Use an X-ray fluorescence (XRF) analyzer in the field to measure the soil Hg, Pb, and As concentrations for each of the four individual soil samples. Note that the XRF can be simultaneously calibrated for additional metals.
- After XRF analysis, combine the four individual soil samples per sampling location into a single composite soil sample. Package and send this composite sample to an accredited laboratory for analysis using guidelines provided by the laboratory for sample preservation, packaging, and shipping. It is recommended that the composite samples be analyzed using inductively coupled plasma–mass spectrometry (ICP-MS) methods, which are considered state-of-the-art for metals analysis (appendix C). Hg will require a separate analysis using cold vapor atomic absorption spectrometry (CVAAS).
- Follow the directions and use the sampling equipment provided or recommended by the in-field research team and analytical laboratory with respect to sample collection, preparation, and shipping (including use of personal protective equipment, such as gloves).
- *Optional:* Due to the specific environmental properties of both Pb and As, the preferred analytical method in soils measures the bioavailable fraction rather than the total fraction of these metals. Bioavailability is important from a risk-assessment perspective since it measures the fraction of an ingested dose that crosses the gastrointestinal epithelium and becomes available for distribution to internal target tissues and organs. Therefore, it is recommended that one quarter (25 percent) and all (100 percent) of targeted samples (for example, homes where milling occurs, schools, playgrounds) be analyzed for bioavailable Pb using EPA Method 1340 (EPA 2017) or similar. Note that, at this time, this method has only been validated for Pb, although it has been used for As (see appendix C). The in-field research team will need to determine whether it is feasible to conduct this extra analysis given possible resource constraints. Appendix C provides more information on sampling methods and links to standards and guidelines.

DUST SAMPLING

Exposure pathways and routes

ASGM activities are likely to result in direct releases of Hg vapors and Pb particulates as well as indirect releases of fugitive dust from contaminated surface soil. The particulates and fugitive dust may contain Hg, Pb, and As, and both adults and children may come into contact with these CoCs. Dermal contact, incidental ingestion, and inhalation of contaminated dust represent important routes and pathways at ASGM sites. Indoor exposures to contaminated dust (the source of which may have been tracked in from outdoors) is of particular concern due to the duration, frequency, and proximity of individuals' contact with indoor surfaces. Dermal exposures can occur when adults or children walk barefoot on dust or when an individual touches the dust (for example, during sleep or play). Incidental ingestion can occur when individuals get dust on their skin (for example, fingers) or an object (for example, a toy), which then comes into contact with their mouth or food. This is a particularly significant exposure pathway for children. Inhalation can occur from direct releases of fugitive dust or when settled dust becomes resuspended (for example, sweeping the floor, wiping surfaces).

Sampling protocol and analysis

Indoor dust samples should be collected at each ASGM and reference site for each household where soil samples are collected as well as the targeted locations where soil samples are collected, if applicable (for example, schools). As was the case for soil sampling, it is important that specific sampling areas within each location be optimized relative to where individuals spend the most time (for example, children's bedroom and living room in homes, classroom or lunchroom at school). Note that outdoor dust samples are of limited utility given the collection of soil samples and are not recommended here.

Typical dust samples are taken on indoor surfaces such as floors, tables, and windowsills. Specific methods for sampling dust at ASGM sites will differ depending on the surface substrate. For dwellings with dirt floors, methods analogous to soil sampling should be used. For dwellings with impervious and smooth surfaces (for example, wood floors, wood tables, and windowsills), wipe samples are preferred. In some instances, vacuum sampling may be required, such as for rough (for example, brick, stone, and so forth) or carpeted surfaces.

Similar to soil sampling, dust samples should undergo two levels of analysis if possible. First, individual dust samples should be analyzed in the field using an XRF analyzer calibrated for Hg, Pb, and As. The XRF can also be simultaneously calibrated for additional metals. Second, composite dust samples should be packaged and sent to an independent (accredited) laboratory for analysis of Hg, Pb, and As. As noted above, other metals may also be evaluated by the analytical laboratory if a multiscreen metals analysis is requested.

When collecting dust samples using the wipe method, the following general guidelines should be followed (box 3.2):

- Collect at least two individual dust samples within each household or indoor location. These locations should be representative of the different indoor areas where the population of interest spends the most time and over which activities occur (for example, bedroom, kitchen, and living room). Different surfaces can be sampled for any given room (for example, floor, table, and windowsill).
- Record all sampling locations on the in-field data sheets.
- The area to be sampled (that is, the area to be wiped) must be a rectangle or square (preferred) with measurable dimensions so the total surface area can be easily calculated, and either marked off with tape or using a cardboard template. It is recommended that the wipe area be at least 900 cm^2 (approximately 1 square foot) to obtain enough dust for analysis of Pb.
- Follow specific guidelines regarding how much pressure to apply on the wipe, how to properly fold the wipe, and what type to wipe to use. The goal is to pick up all dust from the sample area, including any debris (for example, paint chips, chunks of dust or dirt). Disposable, moistened towelettes or baby wipes (for example, GhostWipe™) are generally recommended. The wipe material should meet appropriate performance criteria.
- Use an XRF analyzer in the field to measure the dust Hg, Pb, and As concentrations for each of the individual dust samples. Note that the XRF can be simultaneously calibrated for additional metals, and it may be possible to use the same instrument for both the soil and dust samples, but this will depend on manufacturer specifications.

Important Note
Dust sampling should occur in the same households or locations where other environmental samples are being collected and which relate to individuals providing biomonitoring and health-outcome data.

Example of dust sampling from a hypothetical ASGM site

A total of 267 individual dust samples will be taken from 230 individual households, three elementary schools, four auxiliary processing households, 10 households at which children are known to frequent the primary processing area, and 20 households with known fish consumers. Unlike for soil samples, dust samples will be collected from each household, including the households for which the 10 children work at the primary mining area because (a) there are no indoor areas at the primary processing area, so only soil samples are required; and (b) the children may well be tracking soil into their homes, leading to additional exposures via this pathway. Each composite sample consists of two individual samples per grid location, which are analyzed for Hg, Pb, and As in the field using an XRF analyzer (the composite samples are packaged and sent to an accredited laboratory for analysis of Hg, Pb, and As at a minimum).

- Combine the individual dust samples into a single composite dust sample and package and send this composite sample to an accredited laboratory for analysis.
- Follow the directions and use the sampling equipment provided or recommended by the in-field research team and analytical laboratory with respect to sample collection, preparation, and shipping (including use of personal protective equipment, such as gloves).

WATER SAMPLING

Exposure pathways and routes

ASGM sites have the potential to affect local water supplies due to leaching or runoff of contaminated soil containing metals to surface water or groundwater, leaching of mine tailings to surface water or groundwater, migration of contaminated surface water from wastewater discharges to other surface water sources or groundwater, and dispersion and deposition of Hg vapor to water bodies. Various types of surface-water sources (for example, lakes, rivers, streams) and groundwater sources of various depths may therefore contain Hg, Pb, and As originating from ASGM operations.

Ingestion of and dermal contact with contaminated water are important exposure routes and pathways at ASGM sites. Dermal exposures can occur when adults or children bathe, wash clothes or dishes, swim, or wade in surface-water sources or if groundwater is used for bathing or washing. Direct ingestion can occur when individuals drink water obtained from surface or groundwater sources. Note that either surface water or groundwater (or both) can be used as sources for drinking water at ASGM sites.

As discussed previously, fish and shellfish consumption in communities where this activity is prevalent is likely to be a primary exposure pathway for MeHg, which is formed from environmental methylation of Hg originating from ASGM sites. Although this chapter focuses on household uses of water (for example, drinking and bathing), if fish and shellfish consumption is a significant pathway, then the water body from which fish are collected should also be sampled following these guidelines. Identifying water bodies that serve as both drinking-water sources and fishing activities (either commercial or recreational or both) would allow one set of samples to be used to achieve multiple objectives.

Sampling protocol and analysis

Water samples should be collected at each ASGM and reference site from each household where soil and dust samples were collected, as well as from communal drinking-water sources. Specifically, water samples should be collected at residences, schools, or daycare facilities, and possibly other locations where community members, particularly sensitive subpopulations such as children, spend significant amounts of time and where water is used for drinking, bathing, washing, or recreational purposes. It is important to recognize that the source of drinking water may vary for individuals within a site as well as across ASGM sites, and the collection of drinking-water samples will therefore depend on an understanding of drinking-water sources and population-activity patterns. Typical sources include tap water from a municipal source (groundwater or surface water), an individual, shared household or communal well, a communal surface water source (for example, lake, river, stream), or a communal groundwater well. In some cases, multiple sources will need to be considered.

When collecting water samples, the following general guidelines should be followed (box 3.3):

- If possible, all water samples should be collected at the individual household or dwelling where the water is available for consumption or use. If the source is tap water, water samples should be collected at the point of release (that is, the tap). If the source is surface water or groundwater not accessible via a tap, but which has been transported and stored on-site, water samples should be collected from the location where the water is stored (for example, a container inside home or school). However, in areas with a communal drinking-water source—for example, a community well or surface water body—samples should be collected from the location where community members are obtaining their water. Samples should also be collected directly from an off-site surface water body if it is commonly used for recreational or

Important Note

Water sampling should occur in the same households or locations where other environmental samples are being collected and which relate to individuals providing biomonitoring and health-outcome data.

Box 3.3

Example of water sampling at a hypothetical ASGM site

Water sampling should occur at the water body where fish will be sampled, as well as locations selected based on an assessment of drinking-water sources for those households providing biomonitoring, survey, and health-outcome data. For this example, six individual samples will be collected from the water body at which fishing occurs, with 3 liters to be analyzed using a multi-metal screen and 3 liters analyzed for MeHg. In addition, an analysis of drinking-water sources for the 267 individual households shows that there is no municipal water in this village and that water is typically obtained from 5 different individual sources. Water samples will be collected from each of these 5 locations, for a total of 11 water samples.

other purposes (or if the in-field research team requires additional data on potential site contamination).

- Water samples should reflect the actual water being used for drinking or other purposes; therefore, if the water used within the household has undergone any type of treatment (for example, chlorination), then the treated water should be sampled.
- For each water sample, duplicate samples of approximately one liter each should be taken. The exact sample quantity should be determined together with the laboratory conducting the analyses to ensure laboratory-specific QA/QC requirements are met.
- If the site-specific CSM involves recreational water or fish consumption, water should be collected from those water bodies and analyzed specifically for MeHg.
- Follow the directions and use the sampling equipment provided or recommended by the in-field research team and analytical laboratory with respect to sample collection, preparation, and shipping (including use of personal protective equipment, such as gloves).

FISH-TISSUE SAMPLING

Exposure pathways and routes

The primary CoC released or discharged at ASGM sites into the environment is Hg, which is transformed into MeHg through bacterial methylation in aquatic environments and readily bioaccumulates in the food web. The local population will be exposed to MeHg primarily through fish and shellfish consumption. They may also be exposed via direct contact with contaminated sediments, which typically serve as a reservoir for bioaccumulative contaminants. However, dermal absorption of MeHg is generally low; therefore, sampling sediments is not recommended for evaluating human health exposures unless information obtained by the in-field team suggests otherwise. The exception to that is if it becomes important to model the relationship between sediment MeHg concentrations and fish or shellfish tissue concentrations (for example, use of a bioaccumulation model) in order to predict fish tissue MeHg concentrations under future conditions.

Lead (Pb) does not bio-magnify in fish tissue in the same way as MeHg. That said, there may be measurable concentrations of Pb in fish tissue, but these will be low compared with Pb in soils, dusts, and drinking water. Arsenic (As) does not bioaccumulate in fish as it is transformed to organic As, which has virtually no health implications for fish consumers. Therefore, fish sampling of As and Pb is not recommended unless resources permit such analyses.

SAMPLING PROTOCOL AND ANALYSIS

Rather than sample fish and shellfish from each household, fish should be collected from the water body in which they are caught to provide the range of concentrations that all fish/shellfish consumers are likely to experience and to decrease the overall number of required samples. As noted in box 3.3, targeted sampling of the potentially exposed population (for example, recreational anglers) may be used to identify specific households to include in the sampling program. Alternatively, if there is a commercial fishery, fish may be obtained from these commercial anglers. Determining the specific species to sample and all fish-sampling activities should follow these guidelines:

- Species selection should be informed by identifying the most frequently consumed fish and shellfish from households providing the biomonitoring and health-outcome data. There may be local knowledge (for example, local anglers providing fish for markets) or if fish or shellfish are typically self-caught, then this sampling program may need to incorporate data from the home survey, specifically the food frequency questionnaire (appendix C) to identify specific species. Anecdotal evidence from informal surveys at recreationally fished water bodies may also be used to identify specific households, which can then provide individual samples. In order for the smallest number of samples to provide exposure data for the largest number of participating households, fish samples should be obtained from water bodies used for recreational or commercial fishing that are most likely to have been affected by ASGM activities, focusing on the most frequently consumed species.
- In general, fish at higher trophic levels that forage from sediment-associated food sources will show higher MeHg concentrations than lower-trophic-level fish foraging from water-column sources of food. Thus, the relative trophic level of each species commonly consumed by the local population should also be considered.
- Other important life-history characteristics of preferred fish species for sampling include demersal (that is, bottom-feeding) fish; piscivorous fish (for example, top-level predators that consume other fish); locally resident (for example, non-anadromous species that do not migrate far and demonstrate site fidelity).
- Two different species of 10 individual fish/shellfish each should be collected from each relevant water body (for example, one demersal and one piscivorous).
- Fish should be of a size commonly consumed by individuals or relevant to the food web (for example, forage fish that serve as prey for larger fish).
- For larger fish (for example, generally more than 25 centimeters), typically individual fish will be sampled; but for smaller fish, it is appropriate to analyze composites of a minimum of three individual fish.

Box 3.4

Example of fish sampling at an ASGM site

As noted previously, there is a central water body that is used for recreational fish consumption, and 20 targeted households have been identified as frequent anglers at the water body. Based on information from local anglers as well as the targeted households, the decision is made to sample catfish (demersal) and tiger fish (piscivorous). These are two local favorites that demonstrate site fidelity, are frequently consumed, and have foraging strategies and life histories likely to maximize potential exposures. Ten individual fish (20 total) samples are collected. In addition, 12 individual goby fish (a forage fish likely to be consumed by tiger fish) provide 3 additional composite samples of 6 fish each, for 23 total samples to be analyzed for MeHg.

- At a minimum, analyze for MeHg. Other metals are less likely to bioaccumulate, but a multimetal screen or analysis for other potentially bioaccumulative substances can be conducted if resources allow.
- If bioaccumulation modeling will be conducted, additional fish data will need to be collected to support the modeling effort. A conceptual model of the aquatic food web should first be developed to identify the foraging relationships across species and trophic levels. Additional composite samples of forage fish (which are not typically consumed by people but represent an important exposure to higher-trophic-level fish) will need to be collected to support any efforts to model bioaccumulation.

Sediment sampling

Although the local population may be exposed to metals in sediments through direct contact (for example, swimming, wading, or fishing), expected dermal absorption is low, and this pathway is not typically quantitatively important to overall exposure of MeHg. However, sediment samples may be necessary to inform bioaccumulation modeling. Fish and shellfish are exposed to MeHg primarily through consumption of contaminated prey from MeHg originating in sediments. MeHg concentrations tend to increase with each trophic level, leading to highest concentrations in top-level predatory fish most often consumed by humans. Therefore, it may be necessary to collect sediment samples to effectively model potential exposures to fish.

When collecting sediment samples, the following general guidelines should be used (box 3.5):

- Sediment samples should be collected from areas where fish typically forage. Local anglers will often have information to inform specific sampling locations.
- The exact number of samples will depend on (a) the size of the water body; (b) fish life history and foraging strategies; (c) whether samples will be evaluated for a direct contact (for example, wading) scenario; and (d) whether there is evidence for heterogeneity in expected concentrations.

Important Note

Fish-tissue and sediment sampling should occur from locations where fish are being caught for local consumption by individuals providing biomonitoring and health-outcome data. In the context of linking environmental exposures to health outcomes in an exposed population, there is limited utility to sampling fish that are (a) not being consumed by individuals providing biomonitoring and health-outcome data, and (b) not affected by ASGM activities (for example, beyond the zone of influence of ASGM-waste releases and discharges). Other studies with additional objectives—for example, broader site characterization, more refined modeling, or to evaluate the possibility of contaminated fish being sold or used outside the study area—may benefit from broadening the scope of sampling.

Box 3.5

Example of sediment sampling at an ASGM site

Sediment samples should be collected from the same water body where fish have been sampled and should represent areas that (a) are likely foraging areas for fish—for example, near-shore or fine-grained sediments; and (b) may lead to direct contact exposures from wading—for example, shoreline. At this hypothetical site, 20 individual sampling locations representing 5 discrete areas within the lake have been identified, and these will be evaluated for Hg and Pb in the field using an XRF. Then, 4 individual samples from each of the 5 areas will be composited and sent to a laboratory for MeHg, Hg, and Pb analysis, for a total of 5 laboratory samples.

- Grab sediment samples should only be collected from the top two inches of sediment since this represents the typical active layer to which fish are exposed. However, if additional fate and transport modeling will be conducted, then sediment samples at various depths using a coring instrument will be required in order to better quantify the relationship between deeper and surface sediments.

AGRICULTURAL PRODUCT SAMPLING

Exposure pathways and routes

Because ASGM sites have the potential to affect local soil and water supplies, as discussed above, activities at these ASGM sites may also affect locally produced agricultural products that come into contact with contaminated soil or water. In particular, contaminated irrigation water from affected surface water or groundwater sources may be used to irrigate crops. Crops may also be grown in contaminated soil or subject to aerial deposition, with resulting uptake in root systems or deposition on foliage. Additionally, animals may be grazed on contaminated soil or given contaminated water to drink. Various types of agricultural products may therefore contain Hg, potentially MeHg, given favorable conversion conditions in soil, and Pb and As. Examples of locally produced agricultural products include fruits, vegetables, and grains; animals consumed for meat (for example, chickens, cattle); and various animal products (for example, milk, cheese, eggs). These products may be produced at multiple scales, ranging from small family gardens at the household level to large commercial operations that sell products at local or off-site markets. However, this pathway may not be applicable at all sites depending on specific conditions.

The data on contaminant concentrations in agricultural products (which can include fruits, vegetables, grains, dairy, meat, and eggs) are combined with information on food consumption collected as part of the household survey (chapter 2). Statistical models predicting intake or exploring correlations are used to inform how exposure factors combine with environmental concentrations and how those relate to body burdens from the biomonitoring data. Another approach for this is to analyze food consumption based on a composite sample using a duplicate diet approach. Participants consume food as they normally would over some time period, for example, 24 or 48 hours, making sure to both record what and how much of each food item they are consuming as well as putting aside a small amount of food from each snack and meal. These individual samples are combined into a composite sample and analyzed for CoCs. This method provides detailed information on intake, and when combined with biomonitoring data, can be used to parameterize models that predict CoC concentrations in humans (for example, intake or physiologically based pharmacokinetic [PBPK] models).

Duplicate diet studies are not recommended here since the focus is on exposures occurring over longer time periods. In addition, data on CoC concentrations in agricultural products can be used to estimate population intake rates given assumptions on consumption frequencies and therefore represent more useful data.

Sampling protocol and analysis

Selected agricultural samples should be collected at each ASGM and control site from each household where soil, dust, and water samples have been collected. Specifically, only those agricultural products that are locally grown (either at the household or community level), and which are frequently consumed by the population of interest and have the potential for contamination should be sampled. Determining which specific agricultural products to sample at each site will require further refinement of the conceptual site model (CSM) and a detailed understanding by the in-field research team of the ways in which ASGM activities might affect local resources.

Examples of different types of foodstuffs that might be sampled at individual ASGM sites include the following:

- Rice grown in surface water affected by wastewater from ASGM activities
- Root vegetables grown in soils from backyard gardens irrigated with surface water affected by wastewater from ASGM activities
- Leafy greens grown downwind within a depositional area of ASGM activities
- Beans or other legumes grown in soils contaminated by fugitive dust from ASGM operations or irrigated with contaminated surface water.

When collecting agricultural samples, the following general guidelines should be followed:

- If possible, all agricultural samples should be collected at the individual household where the foodstuff is ready or available for consumption (for example, kitchen), or taken directly from the garden for fruits and vegetables. Samples may be collected from the original source (for example, community field crop) or marketplace for commonly consumed foodstuffs that are not available at the household level (or if the in-field research team requires additional data on potential site contamination). An emphasis should be placed on samples that may be applicable to the largest number of participating households (for example, foods obtained from a market or similar location).
- For samples taken from household gardens, collect multiple samples of the same item if possible and include as a composite sample (for example, a few lettuce leaves from several different heads of lettuce).
- Agricultural samples should reflect only the edible portion of foodstuffs and target those portions of the food of greatest concern (for example, green leaves, chicken liver).
- Sufficient amounts need to be collected per food sample; recommended levels typically range from 40–100 grams for fruits, vegetables, and meat products. The exact amount will depend on the specific laboratory requirements.
- Follow the directions and use the sampling equipment provided or recommended by the in-field research team and analytical laboratory with respect to sample collection, preparation, and shipping (including use of personal protective equipment, such as gloves).

> **Important Note**
>
> Agricultural sampling should occur from the same households or locations where other environmental samples are being collected and which relate directly to individuals providing biomonitoring and health-outcome data. In the context of linking environmental exposures to health outcomes in an exposed population, there is limited utility to sampling products that are (a) not being consumed by individuals providing biomonitoring and health-outcome data; and (b) not affected by ASGM activities (for example, beyond the zone of influence of ASGM-waste releases and discharges). Other studies with additional objectives—for example, broader site characterization, or to evaluate the possibility of contaminated products being sold or used outside the study area—may benefit from broadening the scope of sampling.

REFERENCE

EPA (US Environmental Protection Agency). 2017. "Method 1340: *In Vitro* Bioaccessibility Assay for Lead in Soil." SW-846 Update VI. EPA, Washington, DC.

4 General Guidelines for Biological Sampling

INTRODUCTION

This chapter provides an overview of biological sampling conducted for each participating individual in order to provide data on both internal-exposure concentrations (for example, biomonitoring) and potential health outcomes associated with exposures to the contaminants of concern (CoCs). These data are linked to household- and participant-specific environmental samples collected per the recommendations in chapter 3 and clinical health-outcome data from chapter 5.

Biological samples are used to quantify total exposure to the CoCs at each artisanal small-scale gold mining (ASGM) and reference site from all sources and exposure pathways and routes for each individual. The biological sampling data will also be used to confirm or validate estimates of CoC exposure based on the exposure-factor data (chapter 2) and environmental-sampling data (chapter 3) collected at each site. That is, the goal is to avoid collecting biological samples at future sites if less intrusive exposure-factor and environmental data can be collected that are sufficiently predictive of total exposures. Additionally, as discussed in chapter 5, biological samples will be used to analyze for possible indicators of health outcomes or nutritional and health status.

This chapter provides general guidelines for what types of biological samples should be collected for each contaminant and recommended approaches for sample collection. Important factors that will need to be considered on a site-by-site basis are also noted. Detailed protocols and procedures for collecting a biological sample, handling and preparing biological samples, and laboratory analysis of biological samples are not addressed here and will be the final responsibility of the in-field research team and associated trained professionals (although some useful resources are presented in appendix D). It is essential that the biological sampling be conducted for the same individuals for whom the household survey (chapter 2), environmental (chapter 3), and health-outcome (chapter 5) data are collected. The same type of biological samples should also be collected from both the identified ASGM sites and matched reference sites. Note that any necessary ethical clearances will need to be obtained prior to sample collection by the in-field research team.

The key factors to consider when evaluating potential biomarkers include (a) how well the biomarker correlates with the dose (or external exposure) to appropriate forms of the contaminant (for example, mercury [Hg] versus methylmercury [MeHg]); (b) how well the biomarker correlates with the contaminant concentration in tissue relative to the health outcome; (c) how well the biomarker measurement correlates with changes in the effective dose at the target tissue over time; (d) an understanding of the cultural characteristics of the population; (e) technology availability; and (f) invasiveness of sample collection.

Because the goal of the biological-sampling design is both to (a) quantify the magnitude of exposure among individual population members to each CoC at ASGM sites and (b) identify potential subclinical evidence of diseases that have a high probability of being associated with exposures to these contaminants, the biological sampling should attempt to provide the most accurate and relevant data on biomarkers of exposure or biomarkers of effect for each CoC (and also provide standard information on nutritional and health status). Biological sampling matrices can include urine, blood, toenails, and hair. Breast milk and cord blood are additional matrices but are not recommended in this study due to their limited utility in relating exposure to health outcomes for an infant population. Each of these matrices offers advantages and limitations depending on the contaminant, health outcome or intermediate health outcome, and biomarker to be measured. An emphasis is placed on point-of-care (for example, comparable to in-field for environmental sampling) methods that provide rapid, immunoassay-based results.

BIOLOGICAL SAMPLING MATRICES

Biomarkers of exposure are measurements in biological matrices that reflect the total absorbed or internal dose of a contaminant from all sources and exposure routes and pathways. In some cases, metabolites, as opposed to parent compounds, may provide the most reliable measures of exposure. Biological sampling matrices can include urine, blood, toenails, and hair. Breast milk and cord blood are additional matrices but are not recommended here due to the invasiveness of data collection and limited utility in relating exposure to health outcomes for an infant population. Each of these matrices offers advantages and limitations depending on the contaminant and biomarker to be measured.

The following sections summarize potential biomarkers of exposure specific to each CoC. Because several biological media are possible for each CoC, each of which has advantages and limitations, a hierarchy of preferred options is presented in color-coded tables, as defined in table 4.1.

Biomarkers that can be measured inexpensively using in-field methods are preferred, although there is always a benefit to confirmatory laboratory testing.

Mercury and methylmercury

Hg is the primary CoC at ASGM sites. MeHg may also be a CoC, depending on whether there are affected water bodies as a result of ASGM activities and whether the local population consumes significant amounts of fish or shellfish. Table 4.2 provides an overview of the advantages and limitations of different biological matrices for measuring Hg and MeHg.

TABLE 4.1 **Hierarchy of preferred biomarkers of exposure**

Gold standard. This biomarker has been well vetted in the literature, with one or more validated, cost-effective laboratory methods with high levels of precision. This is the preferred biomarker, given the primary research objectives in this document.

Screening level. This biomarker is an appropriate default for low-resource applications. It is the least invasive, lowest cost, typically with in-field analysis. However, only the total metal can be measured and will have high detection levels and may not have the precision to evaluate statistical associations with outcomes.

Low preference. This biomarker can be used as a last resort but is generally not preferred due to limitations regarding associations (that is, they are not the best measure of exposure or predictive of outcomes based on literature studies).

To be avoided. This biomarker is not appropriate, since it does not measure the exposure of interest, is expensive, or does not have a validated method.

Source: World Bank.
Note: No gray = gold standard; lightest gray = screening level; second-lightest gray = low preference; darkest gray = to be avoided.

TABLE 4.2 **Overview of biomarkers of exposure for Hg and MeHg**

BIOLOGICAL MATRIX AND CONTAMINANT	ADVANTAGES	LIMITATIONS	CAN MATRIX BE USED TO EVALUATE HEALTH OUTCOME?
Inorganic mercury			
Venous blood	Can speciate to determine MeHg, inorganic Hg. Has been widely used in many epidemiological studies.	Invasive (requires venous blood draw); likely reflects more MeHg than inorganic Hg.	Can be used for complete blood count and metabolic panel.
Capillary blood (for example, dried blood spot)	DBS increasingly used in LMIC studies, particularly in newborns; lower cost and less invasive.	Moderately invasive (requires capillary prick).	Can measure hemoglobin, calcium in-field, although not associated with Hg effects.
Urine	Best measure of inorganic Hg, particularly when combined with hair samples. Can measure creatinine.	Moderately invasive (requires urine sample).	Standard renal panel (for example, albumin, protein-uria) as marker for renal damage; creatinine should be measured.
Hair	Not invasive.	80% or more of Hg is MeHg in hair; does not measure inorganic Hg.	No relevant outcome measurement.
Toenail/fingernail	Least invasive and lowest cost if using XRF in-field. Can send to laboratory.	High variability in sample results.	No relevant outcome measurement.
Methylmercury			
Venous blood	Has been used in many epidemiological studies.	Higher cost, more invasive, requires trained professional.	Can be used for complete blood count and metabolic panel.
Capillary blood (for example, dried blood spot)	No in-field analysis method but can send dried blood spot to laboratory.	Method is not fully vetted in the literature; not recommended.	Can measure hemoglobin, calcium in-field, although not associated with MeHg effects.

continued

TABLE 4.2, *continued*

BIOLOGICAL MATRIX AND CONTAMINANT	ADVANTAGES	LIMITATIONS	CAN MATRIX BE USED TO EVALUATE HEALTH OUTCOME?
Urine	No advantages other than less invasive.	Not reliable for MeHg.	Standard renal panel (for example, albumin, protein-uria) as marker for renal damage; can use spot sample.
Hair	Least invasive; relatively low cost. Associated with health outcomes; widely used in epidemiological studies. Can measure total Hg since > 80% is MeHg.	Does not capture inorganic Hg (< 20%).	No relevant outcome measurement.
Toenail/fingernail	No advantages other than less invasive.	Will not distinguish MeHg, Hg in-field. May speciate in laboratory although little evidence in the literature. Not typically used in epidemiological studies.	No relevant outcome measurement.

Source: World Bank.
Note: No gray = gold standard; lightest gray = screening level; second-lightest gray = low preference; darkest gray = to be avoided. Hg = mercury; MeHg = methylmercury.

The most robust biomarker for inorganic Hg is creatinine-adjusted urinary Hg. Urinary Hg concentrations increase as a result of accumulation of inorganic Hg in the kidneys following exposure to Hg vapors during the amalgamation and other ASGM processes, as well as through exposures to dusts and soils with inorganic Hg. For MeHg, proximal hair represents the most informative biomarker that has been consistently used in epidemiological studies and shows a strong association with neurodevelopmental outcomes in children. Proximal hair samples are noninvasive and relatively less expensive than other biological matrices.

As noted above, table 4.2 provides an overview of the advantages and limitations of different biological matrices for sampling Hg and MeHg. The final column is used to identify whether the biological matrix is also useful for evaluating potential biomarkers of effect (chapter 5).

Lead

Lead (Pb) can be an important CoC at ASGM sites, depending on the types of ore that are mined. Whole blood (not serum blood) is the most reliable biological matrix for evaluating Pb exposures. Venous-blood samples collected by a trained medical professional and submitted to an accredited laboratory using inductively coupled plasma–mass spectrometry [ICP-MS] or similar are considered the gold standard for Pb analysis. Somewhat less reliable, but also less invasive, is a dried blood spot collected as a capillary-blood sample in-field and sent to a laboratory.

Finally, an in-field testing instrument (that is, LeadCare Analyzer) calibrated for Pb can be used to collect a capillary-blood sample, with immediate documentation of the results in a computer or on field data sheets, but it is recommended that at least some samples (25 percent) be sent to a laboratory for confirmatory results and to evaluate potential bias, since the in-field method tends to show greater variability and less precision.

The least cost and lowest resource-intensive option involves using an in-field X-ray fluorescence (XRF) analyzer to analyze toenail samples, but detection levels will be higher with greater variability in results. Urine and hair samples are the least reliable biological matrices for evaluating Pb exposures and should generally be avoided for this purpose. Table 4.3 provides an overview of the advantages and limitations of different biological matrices for sampling Pb.

Arsenic

The best measure of As exposure is the metabolite monomethylarsonic acid (percent MMA) obtained from a speciated creatinine-adjusted urine sample. Although this method requires a separate laboratory analysis (for example, high-performance liquid chromatography [HPLC] with hydride atomic absorption spectrometry [HG-AAS] or ICP-MS or similar), it is a widely used measure of exposure in epidemiological studies (it is also more often associated with health outcomes than measures of total As).

An in-field XRF analyzer can be used to analyze toenail samples for As, although there will be greater variability and higher detection levels than with other methods. Blood and hair samples are the least reliable biological matrices for evaluating As exposures and should generally be avoided for this purpose. Table 4.4 provides an overview of the advantages and limitations of different biological matrices for sampling As.

TABLE 4.3 **Overview of biomarkers of exposure for Pb**

BIOLOGICAL MATRIX AND CONTAMINANT	ADVANTAGES	LIMITATIONS	CAN MATRIX BE USED TO EVALUATE HEALTH OUTCOME?
Venous blood	Well-vetted, standardized routine analysis with highest precision and reliability.	Requires medical professional; requirements for processing, storage, handling.	Can do complete blood count and metabolic panel; additional markers related to anemia.
Capillary blood (including dried blood spot)	LeadCare in-field analyzer; immediate results. Alternatively, can use dried blood spot and send to laboratory. Dried blood spot shows high variability compared to venous blood.	Pb only; shows higher variability as compared to venous-blood sample sent to laboratory. Field conditions may compromise ability to measure accurately.	HemoCue in-field for hemoglobin (anemia) as marker of potential intermediate effect. Can measure calcium.
Urine	No advantages other than being less invasive.	Can be used but not preferred.	Standard renal panel (for example, albumin, protein-uria) as marker for renal damage—can use spot sample.
Hair	No advantages other than being less invasive.	Can be used but not preferred; reflects direct contact of hair with dust rather than absorbed exposure.	No relevant outcome measurement.
Toenail/fingernail	Least invasive; lowest cost and immediate results in-field using XRF. No specific storage or transport requirements. Provides information on short- and long-term exposures.	High detection levels. Needs to be correlated with blood levels. LeadCare in-field always preferred.	No relevant outcome measurement.

Source: World Bank.
Note: No gray = gold standard; lightest gray = screening level; second-lightest gray = low preference; darkest gray = to be avoided. XRF = X-ray fluorescence.

TABLE 4.4 **Overview of biomarkers of exposure for As**

BIOLOGICAL MATRIX AND CONTAMINANT	ADVANTAGES	LIMITATIONS	CAN MATRIX BE USED TO EVALUATE HEALTH OUTCOME?
Venous blood	Can use the same sample to evaluate intermediate outcomes.	Not considered reliable; clearance of As is rapid. Time between exposure and sampling is critical. Seafood sources greatly influence blood levels.	Can do complete blood count, assays for precancerous marker (for example, DNA adduct formation, micronucleus formation).
Capillary blood (for example, dried blood spot)	Not as invasive as venous blood; samples can be collected by nonmedical personnel. Storage and transport are significantly simplified.	Still has to be sent to a laboratory; sample volume can be an issue. Not considered reliable for As, given rapid clearance. Time between exposure and sampling is critical. Seafood sources greatly influence levels. Does not show good correlation with split-sample venous blood.	Can measure hemoglobin, calcium in-field, but these have not been associated with As effects.
Urine	Less expensive to measure total As. Can measure multiple metals using the same method.	Total As does not always predict outcomes; associations not statistically significant. May do better collecting toenail.	Standard renal panel (for example, albumin, proteinuria) as marker for renal damage. If collecting for speciated As, then only requires small additional volume. Can also use spot sample or dipstick.
Speciated urine	Percent MMA shows consistent relationship with lung, skin, bladder cancer from oral exposures. Can use same sample for standard renal panel; creatinine.	More expensive than total As; analysis is unique to As.	
Hair	No advantages other than less invasive.	Does not reflect internal/absorbed dose; reflects external exposures.	No relevant outcome measurement.
Toenail/fingernail	Least invasive, lowest cost and immediate results in-field if using XRF. No specific storage or transport requirements. Provides information on short- and long-term exposures.	High detection levels. Measures total As. Random within-person exposure variability leads to attenuation of measures of association between exposure and outcome.	No relevant outcome measurement.

Source: World Bank.
Note: No gray = gold standard; lightest gray = screening level; second-lightest gray = low preference; darkest gray = to be avoided. As = arsenic; MMA = metabolite monomethylarsonic acid; XRF = X-ray fluorescence.

SAMPLING PROTOCOL

Biological samples collected in-field and being sent to a laboratory should be collected by a trained professional. If a medical examination will be conducted for evaluating health outcomes, then a medical professional should collect these samples (chapter 5). Standardized guidelines exist for collecting biological samples.

(For relevant resources related to biomonitoring, including recommended methods and guidance from health agencies, specific testing protocols, and examples of specific guidelines from the US Centers for Disease Control and Prevention, World Health Organization, and others, see appendix D.)

When collecting and analyzing biological samples, the following general guidelines should be followed:

- When collecting blood samples, particularly capillary-blood samples, the skin must first be thoroughly washed and dried to avoid contamination. This is a common problem encountered during field studies of this kind.
- If collecting a dried blood spot, discard the first drop. Contamination is very likely when collecting these samples. Follow all laboratory guidelines and protocols.
- When collecting toenail samples, it may be possible to use the same XRF analyzer as is used for soil and dust sampling, but this instrument will require a separate calibration and samples cannot be collected simultaneously. Thus, it may be more appropriate to have dedicated XRF devices for specific purposes.
- When collecting urine samples, the first morning void is preferred because it is generally more concentrated. This will require some planning to obtain a sample during this time period. Note that 24-hour urine samples may be too cumbersome to collect and spot urine samples may be less robust.
- If the same venous-blood or urine samples will be used to assess indicators of nutrient status or health outcomes, greater sample volumes of whole blood or urine may be needed.
- For both blood and urine samples, stringent guidelines related to the preservation and transportation of biological samples must be followed.
- Urine samples should be adjusted for creatinine levels to account for dilution-dependent sample variation in urine concentrations (that is, individuals who are well hydrated will have more diluted urinary concentrations of environmental contaminants).

5 General Guidelines for Health-Outcomes Assessment

INTRODUCTION

This chapter provides general guidelines for collecting health-outcome data based on a combination of possible approaches, including self-reported health status and medical histories that can be administered by nonmedical personnel, medical examinations, and biological sampling conducted by health professionals, and diagnostic-screening tools related to specific health outcomes that might be administered by a physician or psychologist. The exact approach to be followed at each site will depend on participant access to health-care facilities (where examinations and screenings are likely to occur); availability of in-field methods (for surveys, exams, sample collection, or other tools that can be implemented onsite); and researcher access to validated culturally sensitive diagnostic tools.

Health-outcome data will be collected from individuals within the households identified for sampling in chapter 2. The same health-outcome data should be collected from individuals in both the identified artisanal small-scale gold-mining (ASGM) sites and matched reference sites to evaluate differences that may be attributable to differences in exposures to contaminants of concern (CoCs). Note that any necessary ethical and Institutional Review Board (IRB) clearances will need to be obtained prior to data collection.

There are three measurable categories of possible health outcomes:

- The first is a medical diagnosis related to direct or measurable clinical outcomes known to be associated with exposure to the CoC of interest—for example, bladder cancer or hyperkeratosis associated with arsenic (As) exposures; cognitive deficits as measured by age-specific standardized testing instruments associated with exposures to methylmercury (MeHg), lead (Pb), and As.
- The second is an intermediate, nonspecific observation or measurement associated with the health outcome of interest (for example, increased blood pressure associated with cardiovascular outcomes that may be related to exposure to Pb and MeHg).
- The third is an intermediate biochemical measurement (that is, biomarker of effect) that requires laboratory or in-field analysis of a biological matrix

(for example, diagnosis of anemia based on hematocrit level in blood that may be related to Pb exposures or micronucleus formation in blood that may be associated with genotoxic effects of As).

It should be noted that biomonitoring is a rapidly expanding field with improvements in molecular techniques leading to the identification of novel biomarkers, including oncogenes, tumor-suppressor genes, micro-RNAs and long noncoding RNAs, DNA methylation, and others. The evolving discipline of "omics," including proteomics and genomics, has led to the identification of genetic and epigenetic alterations, typically based on blood samples and utilizing various laboratory-based assays. These methods are not mature enough yet to recommend for routine use in low- and middle-income countries (LMICs) but could be considered in the future. Key current drawbacks are the requirement for specialized laboratory equipment, the invasiveness of biological sampling (typically a venous-blood sample is required), and the increased expense of such analyses.

Although it would be desirable to measure unique health outcomes associated with exposures to each CoC from one or more of these categories, a key challenge of this type of investigation is that the primary CoCs (for example, mercury [Hg], MeHg, Pb, and As) from ASGM sites as well as other factors share common biological targets, so it is difficult to discern the relative contribution (if any) of each CoC exposure to the identified health outcome. For example, exposure to multiple CoCs has been associated with cognitive and neurodevelopmental outcomes in children using age-specific standardized instruments (such as the Bayley Scale of Infant and Toddler Development and IQ tests).

Additionally, intermediate measures of health outcomes in the absence of overt toxicity (biomarkers of effect) may show associations with exposure concentrations as measured through biomonitoring (chapter 4) or environmental concentrations of CoCs (chapter 3). Therefore, it is important to note that while biomarkers of exposure are CoC-specific, biomarkers of effect may not be CoC-specific. Moreover, there are many other factors that could influence the same health outcomes associated with these CoCs, ranging from such lifestyle factors as diet, exercise, and smoking status to common environmental exposures, such as air pollution. It is anticipated that these latter factors will be captured during the household survey and subsequently controlled for through statistical analyses of the data.

Given these constraints, the primary goal of these guidelines is to try to collect enough information about direct and indirect health outcomes from each participant to evaluate (a) differences in these outcomes between the ASGM-exposed population and a nonexposed reference population; and (b) possible relationships between measured environmental concentrations (chapter 3), biomarkers of exposure (chapter 4), and health outcomes at the individual level.

SELF-REPORTED HEALTH STATUS AND MEDICAL HISTORY

Each participant should provide basic health-related information, including the following:

- Age, weight, body-mass index
- Smoking status

- Alcohol consumption
- Physical activity
- Medication use (for example, antihypertensive)
- Medical diagnoses and dates of diagnosis, including high blood pressure, such chronic illnesses as cancer or kidney disease, or any other medical or mental health conditions. If the medical history is for a child under the age of 18, a parent or caregiver will likely need to provide this information.
- Health status relative to any known deficiencies (for example, rickets and pyorrhea), particularly in children
- Past and present illnesses, whether formally diagnosed or not, and dates and information on any serious or chronic illnesses the person has experienced; for instance, if the individual has ever had tuberculosis or if the individual has asthma or diabetes
- Family medical history, such as information on any diagnosed health conditions of immediate family members (for example, parents or siblings), including such conditions as cancer, heart disease, and mental illness.

This information can be obtained in-field as part of the household survey (see appendix B and the Sample Home Survey Questionnaire questions starting with number four). Alternatively, if a medical examination will be conducted, a more complete medical history can be obtained under the supervision of a medical professional, which is likely to provide more detailed and refined data based on clinical observations. See, for example, resources such as *Bates' Guide to Physical Examination and History Taking,* 13th ed. (Bickley et al. 2021).

Medical exams and biological testing

Selected health outcomes can be measured using direct observation or testing, some of which may be accomplished by nonmedical personnel in the field (for example, blood pressure), while other health outcomes (for example, arsenicosis versus a generalized skin rash) may require specific training for nonmedical professionals or even a more formal medical diagnosis.

Biological sampling may also provide useful information about potential health impacts or precursor effects. *Biomarkers of effect* are measurements in biological matrices that (a) serve as an indicator of a specific health outcome or preclinical (upstream) change or effect at the molecular or cellular level, or (b) have been shown to reliably predict health outcomes. These measurements are typically obtained from standard blood or urine tests, such as a complete blood count (CBC) or a standard renal panel. Although most biomarkers of effect are nonspecific with respect to exposure (that is, it is not possible to discern the source of the observed biomarker or whether it is attributed to the contaminants of interest), they can serve as potential indicators for the health outcome of interest. However, it is important to recognize that upstream or precursor effects may not lead to downstream outcomes or permanent effects. Biomarkers of effect can therefore provide useful (although not definitive) information and indicators on the continuum from exposure to overt health outcome. Table 5.1 provides an overview of the recommended biomarkers of effect (including nutritional and health status), with an emphasis on lower-cost, point-of-care approaches, followed by a discussion of each proposed biomarker by category of health outcome.

TABLE 5.1 Overview of recommended biomarkers of effect

BIOMARKER	SAMPLING APPROACH	PURPOSE	NOTES
Proteinuria	Reagent strip point-of-care testing device; dipstick	Renal effects; specifically recommended as part of CIMI toolkit (chapter 4)	Total protein in urine
Albumin	Reagent strip point-of-care testing device; dipstick	Renal effects; microalbuminuria noted as sensitive biomarker with respect to renal outcomes	Predominant protein found in urine
Creatinine	Requires urine sample (no dipstick)	Necessary to adjust for urine volume	
25hydroxyvitamin D_3 $(25(OH)D_3)$	May be possible in field	Vitamin D deficiency, micronutrient status	Vemulapati et al. 2017.
Calcium		Health status, micronutrient status	
Hemoglobin	In-field HemoCue	Measures anemic status; associated with Pb, also absorption of metals	Complete blood count from a venous sample provides additional markers such as hematocrit, platelet count, corpuscular volume, and so forth.
C-reactive protein	Dried blood spot; may be a rapid point-of-care method	Associated with lung health (As) and cardiovascular outcomes (Pb)	See appendix D for references and links to point-of-care CRP methods.
DNA adduct formation	Should be possible to use dried blood spot sent to lab	Associated with carcinogenic outcomes (As)	Recommended by the International Programme on Chemical Safety (IPCS)
Micronucleus formation	Should be possible to use dried blood spot sent to lab	Associated with carcinogenic outcomes (As)	Recommended by the IPCS

Source: World Bank.
Note: As = arsenic; CIMI = chronic inorganic mercury intoxication; CRP = C-reactive protein; Pb = lead.

Renal effects

Urinary and serum enzymes and low molecular weight (LMW) proteins have been used as early markers of kidney dysfunction and are useful for the detection of small changes in the function of tubular epithelial cells predictive of many pathological conditions. Enzyme and protein excretion increases before elevation of other markers of renal function, such as creatinine, and well before overt disease. Enzyme-excretion rates in urine or blood are elevated following release from cells damaged by exposure to exogenous substances such as CoCs, or from regenerating cells that lead to increased enzyme induction. LMW proteins are freely filtered across the glomerular capillary wall and almost completely reabsorbed by the proximal tubular cells. Functional or structural damage from exposure to CoC can lead to reduced reabsorption in the proximal tubule, leading to increases in proteins in both blood and urine. These biomarkers are associated with exposures to cadmium (Cd) and Pb.

Proteinuria is a classic early sign of kidney dysfunction and although reversible, its presence carries important prognostic information. Proteinuria is typically measured as total protein and can be evaluated using a rapid in-field reagent strip in a spot-urine sample. Early-morning void is preferred, and urinary creatinine should be measured concurrently. Validated in-field or "point-of-care" assays exist; however, sending urine samples to a laboratory for a standard renal panel will always yield more information—for example, albumin, BUN (blood urea nitrogen)/creatinine ratio (calculated), calcium, carbon dioxide, chloride, creatinine, estimated glomerular filtration rate (calculated), glucose, phosphate, potassium, and sodium. Proteinuria can be measured as total protein or albumin (microalbuminuria), which is shown to be an excellent predictor of kidney function and is the preferred biomarker.

Cardiovascular effects

Potential cardiovascular effects associated with exposure to CoCs found at ASGM sites can vary from atherosclerosis to myocardial infarction to ischemic events broadly referred to as cardiovascular disease (CVD). C-reactive protein (CRP) is a blood biomarker of inflammation shown to be predictive of a range of cardiovascular outcomes. While not as sensitive or as specific as homocysteine, CRP can be measured using in-field assays and has also been shown to be predictive of chronic kidney disease and chronic obstructive pulmonary disease (COPD). Individuals with COPD face a two-to-five-times greater risk of developing lung cancer, a key outcome associated with As exposures. Thus, CRP, while nonspecific, may be indicative of intermediate health outcomes associated with exposure to CoCs at ASGM sites.

Recently, bioactive molecules—such as asymmetric dimethylarginine (ADMA) and adipocyte fatty acid-binding protein (FABP4, also known as aP2 and AFABP)—have emerged as new predictive biomarkers of CVD and have also been associated with blood Pb levels. In the future, these may be considered in lieu of CRP. For related information, see McDonnell et al. (2009).

Carcinogenic effects

Exposures to As are associated with carcinogenic outcomes, including lung, skin, and kidney cancers. Although the Sample Home Survey Questionnaire (appendix B) includes a set of questions on health status, it is unlikely that enough cases will be observed to draw statistically meaningful conclusions, particularly given the emphasis on selecting children from each participating household (chapter 2). Therefore, a potential biomarker in the absence of disease may be indicative of changes at the cellular level that are predictive of carcinogenic outcomes.

The International Programme on Chemical Safety has published guidelines to provide concise guidance on the planning, performing, and interpretation of studies to monitor groups or individuals exposed to genotoxic agents. Based on those guidelines, DNA-adduct formation or micronucleus formation are two standardized assays that provide important prognostic information on exposure to potential carcinogens such as As.

CoC-specific health outcomes

The following subsections describe the primary health outcomes associated with each CoC and recommended methods for evaluating them using medical exams and biological sampling. Appendix A provides a brief toxicity profile for each CoC, as well as links to detailed toxicological profiles developed by the US Environmental Protection Agency, World Health Organization, and others.

Mercury and methylmercury

One of the earliest health outcomes associated with exposure to Hg is neurotoxicity, including tremors and ataxia, for example, as measured by the chronic inorganic mercury intoxication (CIMI) toolkit. By contrast, exposures to MeHg are associated with neurodevelopmental and cognitive outcomes, particularly in children, as measured by age-specific, standardized testing instruments. At ASGM sites, it is likely that the general population will be exposed to several forms of Hg via different pathways; namely, elemental Hg vapor in air, inorganic Hg in soil, and MeHg from local fish (if relevant). A careful analysis may be able to identify proportional contributions from each of these sources using a combination of environmental sampling data (chapter 3) together with biomonitoring data (chapter 4) and metrics related to health outcomes (this chapter), but this will require additional data collection (for example, speciation in biological matrices).

However, a simpler, less resource-intensive analysis can be conducted that will provide insight into the relationship between Hg exposures regardless of speciation and health outcomes overall. Specifically, Doering, Bose-O'Reilly, and Berger (2016) developed the CIMI toolkit based on data and analyses conducted under the Global Mercury Project from several ASGM sites in Indonesia, the Philippines, Tanzania, and Zimbabwe. The goal was to develop a rapid but reliable assessment tool to identify a streamlined set of indicators based on symptoms and observations to diagnose the degree of chronic inorganic mercury intoxication based on a combined score that is applicable to both children and adults. The indicators are shown in table 5.2.

TABLE 5.2 **CIMI indicators**

INDICATOR	MEASUREMENT APPROACH
Self-reported symptoms	
Excessive salivation	Self-reported through the household survey (appendix B, questions 4+) or as part of a medical history
Tremors throughout the day	
Trouble sleeping at night	
Clinical observations	
Gray-to-bluish gum discoloration	In-field observation as part of household survey or formal medical diagnosis
Heel-to-shin ataxia	With the participant lying supine, instruct the participant to place their right heel on their left shin just below the knee and then slide it down their shin to the top of their foot. Have them repeat this motion as quickly as possible without making mistakes. Have the participant repeat this movement with the other foot. An inability to perform this motion in a relatively rapid cadence is abnormal. This may be performed by an appropriately trained in-field team but would benefit from a medical professional.
Dysdiadochokinesis (rapidly alternating movement evaluation)	Ask the participant to place their hands on their thighs and then rapidly turn their hands over and lift them off their thighs. Once the patient understands this movement, tell them to repeat it rapidly for 10 seconds. Normally this is possible without difficulty. This may be performed by an appropriately trained in-field team but would benefit from a medical professional.
Walking (gait) ataxia	Observe the participant walk across the room under observation. Gross gait abnormalities should be noted. Next ask the participant to walk heel to toe across the room, then on their toes only, and finally on their heels only. Normally, these maneuvers are possible without too much difficulty.
	Be certain to note the amount of arm swinging because a slight decrease in arm swinging is a highly sensitive indicator of upper extremity weakness. Finally, hop in place on each foot.

continued

TABLE 5.2, *continued*

INDICATOR	MEASUREMENT APPROACH
Proteinuria	See chapter 5 on biomonitoring. This is measured in a laboratory or using rapid in-field assay.
Neuropsychological testing	
Pencil-tapping test (tremor and coordination)	Ask the participant to tap as many dots as possible on a piece of paper in 10 seconds. Record the number of dots for each participant. This may be performed by an appropriately trained in-field team but would benefit from a medical professional.
Matchbox test (coordination, tremor, and concentration)	Twenty matches are outside an empty matchbox 15 cm away on both sides. Ask the participant to put the matches back in the box and record the amount of time it takes. This may be performed by an appropriately trained in-field team but would benefit from a medical professional.

Source: World Bank.

Recommendations:

- Administer the CIMI as presented in table 5.2 to each participant (can be done in-field with appropriately trained personnel or as part of a more formal clinical assessment).
- Conduct age-specific, culturally relevant cognitive testing for each child.
- Measure proteinuria.

Lead

The key health outcomes associated with exposure to Pb include cognitive and neurodevelopmental effects in children as demonstrated through performance on age-specific, culturally relevant standardized testing instruments (see section below on neurodevelopmental and neurotoxic outcomes).

A secondary, nonspecific health outcome for Pb includes impacts on the renal system, which can be evaluated using nonspecific biomarkers of effect measured using in-field approaches, at a minimum, and sent to a laboratory for the most reliable, precise results. These impacts on the renal system may ultimately lead to cardiovascular outcomes. A key, nonspecific risk factor for cardiovascular outcomes that may also reflect increasing renal damage is blood pressure, which is easy to measure in the field or at a health care facility. In addition, there are related biomarkers that are predictive of clinical health outcomes and associated with intermediate outcomes, including CRP and protein in the urine (proteinuria; typically measured using albumin levels). Anemic status is also significant and can be measured using in-field methods such as HemoCue. Anemia may be related to health outcomes and may also influence Pb absorption.

Recommendations:

- Measure blood pressure in adults in the field or as part of a medical examination.
- Measure specific biomarkers including proteinuria (for example, albumin, ALA); anemia status (for example, hematocrit); cardiovascular risk (for example, CRP).
- Conduct age-specific, culturally relevant cognitive testing for each child (see section below).

Arsenic

Exposure to As has been associated with a number of health outcomes, including skin cancer, bladder cancer, lung cancer, neurodevelopmental health outcomes in children, and arsenicosis. Because skin is a primary target for As, hyperpigmentation and hyperkeratosis can be an early symptom of As exposures and are often first seen on the feet, hands, and palms. Figure 5.1 provides an overview of the primary dermatological signs and symptoms induced by As.

Table 5.3 provides an overview of the health outcomes that have been associated with exposure to As and preferred assessment methods.

Recommendations:

- Conduct age-specific, culturally relevant cognitive testing for each child.
- Conduct in-field screening for keratosis on the soles of the feet as part of the household survey (appendix B) or as part of a more formal medical examination.
- If keratosis is observed, consider a carcinogenic biomarker such as DNA-adduct or micronucleus-formation assay.
- Measure CRP as a nonspecific biomarker of intermediate effects.

Diagnostic screening tools

As with biomarkers of effect, there are nonunique health outcomes that may be indicative of exposure to CoCs and apply to more than one CoC. For example,

FIGURE 5.1

Dermatological outcomes associated with As exposures

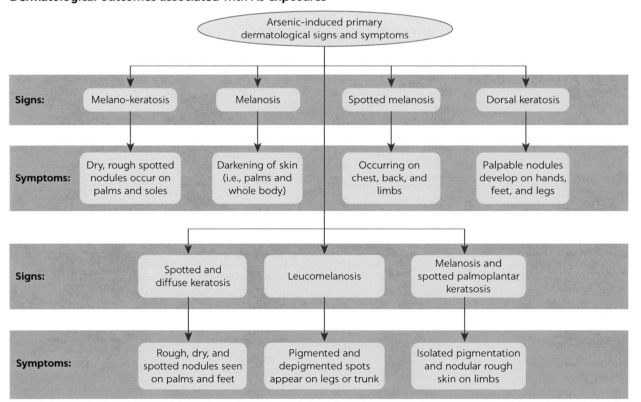

Source: Adapted from Abdul et al. 2015.

TABLE 5.3 **Health outcomes associated with As exposures**

HEALTH OUTCOME	INTERMEDIATE HEALTH OUTCOME OR DIAGNOSTIC TEST	NONSPECIFIC BIOMARKER OF EFFECT
Arsenicosis: Precursor of squamous cell carcinoma in adults; may be present in children	Keratosis on the soles of the feet	Not applicable
Lung cancer	Lung-function tests	DNA-adduct formation; micronucleus formation
Chronic obstructive pulmonary disease	Lung-function tests	C-reactive protein (CRP); predictor of forced expiratory volume
Heart disease (in adults)	Blood pressure	CRP
Cognitive and neurodevelopmental effects in children	Age-specific, culturally relevant standardized test	Not applicable

Source: World Bank.
Note: As = arsenic.

exposure to MeHg, Hg, Pb, and As has been associated with neurodevelopmental health outcomes in children as measured by standardized tests.

Pulmonary function testing (PFT)

Lung cancer is a known health outcome associated with As exposures. While it may not be possible to observe cancer cases, particularly in young participants, simple lung-function tests that can be administered in-field may suggest impacts to the lung that indicate increased risk of other outcomes. Decreased lung function may be an intermediate indicator of exposures to As and may provide an indication of increased risk of other adverse health outcomes. Standard lung-function tests are noninvasive tests that show how well the lungs are working. The following standardized tests measure lung volume, capacity, rates of flow, and gas exchange:

- Tidal volume (VT): This is the amount of air inhaled or exhaled during normal breathing.
- Minute volume (MV): This is the total amount of air exhaled per minute.
- Vital capacity (VC): This is the total volume of air that can be exhaled after inhaling as much as possible.
- Functional residual capacity (FRC): This is the amount of air left in lungs after exhaling normally.
- Residual volume: This is the amount of air left in the lungs after exhaling as much as possible.
- Total lung capacity: This is the total volume of the lungs when filled with as much air as possible.
- Forced vital capacity (FVC): This is the amount of air exhaled forcefully and quickly after inhaling as much as possible.
- Forced expiratory volume (FEV): This is the amount of air expired during the first, second, and third seconds of the FVC test.
- Forced expiratory flow (FEF): This is the average rate of flow during the middle half of the FVC test.
- Peak expiratory flow rate (PEFR): This is the fastest rate that air can be forced out of the lungs.

A variety of inexpensive peak-flow meters (one size for younger children and a larger size for older children and adults) exists to measure FEV, FVC, and FEF. Flow meters can be utilized in the field and do not require a medical professional but do require training prior to use. The following guidelines are based on best practices:

- Before each use of the meter, make sure the sliding marker or arrow is at the bottom of the numbered scale (for example, zero or the lowest number on the scale).
- Make sure the participant is standing up straight and have the participant remove gum or any food from his or her mouth. Have the participant take in as deep a breath as possible and put the peak-flow meter in his or her mouth. Make sure his or her tongue is not on the mouthpiece. In one breath, have the participant blow out as hard and as quickly as possible. This should not be a slow exhale but rather a fast, hard blast until nearly all of the air has been removed from the lungs.
- The force of the air exhaled from the lungs causes the marker to move along the numbered scale. Record the number.
- Repeat the entire routine three times. In general, when all three exhalations are relatively close, this is an indication that the test is being performed correctly.
- Record the highest of the three results. Do not calculate an average. It is never possible to breathe out too much when using the peak flow meter, but it is possible to exhale too little.

Recommendations:

- Measure FEV, FVC, and FEF for each participant using a peak-flow meter—can be done in-field.
- Measure CRP, an inflammation biomarker predictive of FEV and respiratory, cardiovascular, and renal outcomes.

Neurodevelopmental and neurotoxic outcomes

A key outcome of exposure to Hg, MeHg, Pb, and to some extent As includes neurodevelopmental and cognitive health impacts, particularly in young children, as well as neurotoxicity across the lifespan. Depending on which area of the central nervous system and brain is most affected, there will be differences in the predominant effect. For example, as noted earlier, exposure to Hg is associated with neurotoxicity, including tremors, ataxia, and motor effects. In children, this translates to testing protocols that focus on motor development, including the matchbox test, which measures how long it takes to put 20 matches into a box using alternating hands, and the pencil-tapping test, which measures how many dots children can tap onto a piece of paper in 10 seconds. By contrast, exposures to MeHg and Pb tend to be neurodevelopmental and cognitive, which involves a different set of diagnostic tests.

Methods to assess child development include the following:

- Direct assessment using standardized approaches by a trained medical professional in a clinical environment
- Verbal reporting or completion of a questionnaire by parents or teachers
- Unstructured observation by a trained professional in a familiar environment (for example, at home or school).

Direct assessment using standardized approaches is the preferred approach, since parental reporting may be subject to recall bias. Unstructured observation, although carried out by a professional, is difficult to reproduce, interpret, and compare to other results.

Direct assessment using standardized tests is used to evaluate a range of outcomes, including cognitive development; expressive and receptive language; fine and gross motor development (generally more associated with Hg exposures than MeHg and Pb); academic performance (for example, math and reading comprehension); and intelligence quotient (IQ). The specific approach chosen depends on the availability of a culturally appropriate, age-specific instrument given the age and native language of the individual being tested. Results are scaled to a standardized, normative metric. Results can also be expressed as percentile ranks relative to the standardization sample. In general, normative populations for neurodevelopmental tests have been based on Western or developed countries, which are of limited utility in an LMIC context. Developmental assessments of children in LMICs face challenges due to socioeconomic, cultural, and language differences in the populations being tested. This leads to the necessity for adapting tests designed for one context and makes it difficult to compare results across countries.

The testing protocol that is selected must demonstrate internal consistency, interobserver agreement, test-retest reliability, sensitivity to maturational changes, and the ability to identify relevant outcomes. These tests must be administered by trained medical professionals (for example, child psychologists). Therefore, it is important to select a testing protocol that has been validated for the context in which it is being applied. In 2017, the World Bank published a toolkit that provides a practical "how-to" guide for selection and adaptation of child development measurements for use in LMICs (Fernald et al. 2017). The toolkit proposes a step-by-step process to select, adapt, implement, and analyze early childhood development data. The Early Childhood Development (ECD) Measurement Inventory that accompanies the toolkit contains 147 measurement tools for children under 18. For each test, it reports the domains assessed, age range for which the tool is appropriate, method of administration, purpose of the assessment, origin and locations of use, logistics, and cost. This guide, and other, similar guides (discussed in appendix E) should be consulted in conjunction with a trained professional as part of the in-field research team (for example, Fernald et al. 2017).

The following guidelines should be considered in selecting which testing protocol to use:

- Consultation with a medical professional with demonstrated experience in LMIC settings. It is important to include a researcher with experience in administering neurodevelopmental tests, particularly in an LMIC context. Familiarity with specific testing protocols should be emphasized.
- Time availability and conditions under which testing is to be conducted. A key consideration is how much time will be made available to administer each test. In general, a comprehensive battery of neurodevelopmental testing takes several hours and requires a clinical setting (for example, quiet, no distractions, stress-free, and so forth).
- Cultural relevance. The test must be appropriate for the cultural context and age of the child, as well as acceptability of the test to the local population.

- Availability of normative data. The testing protocol should have a standardized, normative reference to evaluate the results in a consistent and comparable way.
- Consideration of comorbidities. Stress, malnutrition, and nutritional status generally; low socioeconomic status; maternal education; and general household culture (for example, excessive alcohol use, smoking, drugs, and so forth) have all been associated with performance on developmental tests. These should be noted as part of the background information on the individual being tested.

Recommendations:

- Age-specific, culturally relevant cognitive testing for each child
- Pencil-tapping and matchbox test (part of CIMI) for each child and adult

Appendix E provides additional resources and weblinks for assessing health outcomes.

REFERENCES

Abdul, K. S., S. S. Jayasinghe, E. P. Chandana, C. Jayasumana, and P. M. De Silva. 2015. "Arsenic and Human Health Effects: A Review." *Environmental Toxicology and Pharmacology* 40 (3): 828–46.

Bickley, L. S., P. G. Szilagyi, R. M. Hoffman, and Rainier P. Soriano. 2021. *Bates' Guide to Physical Examination and History Taking.* 13th ed. Philadelphia: Wolters Kluwer.

Doering, S., S. Bose-O'Reilly, and U. Berger. 2016. "Essential Indicators Identifying Chronic Inorganic Mercury Intoxication: Pooled Analysis across Multiple Cross-Sectional Studies." *PLoS ONE* 11 (8): e0160323. doi:10.1371/journal.pone.0160323.

Fernald, L. C. H., E. Prado, P. Kariger, and A. Raikes. 2017. "A Toolkit for Measuring Early Childhood Development in Low- and Middle-Income Countries." Prepared for the Strategic Impact Evaluation Fund. Washington, DC: World Bank.

McDonnell, B., S. Hearty, P. Leonard, and R. O'Kennedy. 2009. "Cardiac Biomarkers and the Case for Point-of-Care Testing." *Clinical Biochemistry* 42 (7–8): 549–61.

Vemulapati, S, E. Rey, D. O'Dell, S. Mehta, and D. Erickson. 2017. "A Quantitative Point-of-Need Assay for the Assessment of Vitamin D_3 Deficiency." *Scientific Reports* 7 (1): 14142.

APPENDIX A

Overview of Contaminants

ELEMENTAL MERCURY, INORGANIC MERCURY (Hg)

Sources

Elemental Hg is liquid at room temperature. It is used in some thermometers, dental amalgams, fluorescent light bulbs, mining, and some electrical switches and industrial processes. It is released into the air during the burning of fossil fuels including coal. Inorganic Hg compounds are formed when Hg combines with other elements, such as sulfur or oxygen, to form compounds or salts. Inorganic Hg compounds can occur naturally in the environment but are also used in some industrial processes and in the making of other chemicals. Outside the United States, inorganic Hg salts have been used in cosmetic skin creams.

Health outcomes

Exposure to Hg is associated with neurological, kidney, and autoimmune effects. Chronic, low-level exposures lead to gingivostomatitis, photophobia, tremors, and such neuropsychiatric symptoms as fatigue, insomnia, anorexia, shyness, withdrawal, depression, nervousness, irritability, and memory problems. Exposure to Hg vapors can quickly cause severe lung damage. At low vapor concentrations over a long time, neurological disturbances, memory problems, skin rash, and kidney abnormalities may occur. When repeatedly applied to the skin over long period of time, inorganic Hg compounds will cause similar effects as Hg vapor exposure, including neurological disturbances, memory problems, skin rashes, and kidney abnormalities.

TABLE A.1 **Additional information and detailed profiles on mercury**

SOURCE	DESCRIPTION
ATSDR (US Agency for Toxic Substances and Disease Registry). 1999. "Toxicological Profile for Mercury." Atlanta: ATSDR.	Links to ATSDR toxicological profiles as well as community resources and other resources for health professionals, https://www.atsdr.cdc.gov/toxprofiledocs/
EA (Environment Agency). 2009. "Soil Guideline Values for Mercury in Soil." Science Report SC050021/Mercury SGV. Bristol, UK: EA.	Contains toxicological information and describes environmental fate and exposure pathways
Concise International Chemical Assessment Documents (CICADs), published by the World Health Organization (WHO) within the framework of the International Programme on Chemical Safety (IPCS) and with the cooperation of the International Labour Organization (ILO) and United Nations Environment Programme (UNEP).	CICADs join the IPCS's Environmental Health Criteria documents (EHCs) as authoritative documents on the risk assessment of chemicals. They provide detailed toxicological profiles.
WHO, UNEP, and IOMC (World Health Organization, United Nations Environment Programme, and Inter-Organization Programme for the Sound Management of Chemicals). 2008. "Guidance for Identifying Populations at Risk from Mercury Exposure." Guide and reference document. Geneva: WHO and UNEP.	Includes guidelines and numerous resources (food-frequency questionnaire, cognitive testing) on Hg, inorganic Hg, and MeHg

Source: World Bank compilation.

METHYLMERCURY (MeHg)

Sources

Organic Hg compounds are formed when Hg combines with carbon. Once Hg has been emitted, MeHg is formed from methylation of Hg in sediments in wetlands, rivers, estuaries, and other aquatic environments as a result of microscopic organisms in water and soil. Once methylation has occurred, MeHg readily accumulates in aquatic food webs, starting with benthic (sediment-associated) and pelagic (water-column-associated) organisms serving as prey base for forage fish and ultimately large predatory fish typically consumed by humans. Thimerosal and phenylmercuric acetate are other types of organic Hg compounds made in small amounts for use as preservatives.

Health outcomes

Due to MeHg having greater lipid solubility than Hg has, some 90 percent of MeHg is absorbed into the bloodstream via the gastrointestinal tract. MeHg readily crosses the blood-brain barrier and accumulates in the central nervous system. The peripheral nervous system and kidneys can also be affected. Symptoms of neurologic disease associated with MeHg exposure include tingling in the extremities, headaches, ataxia, dysarthria, visual-field constriction, blindness, hearing impairment, and psychiatric disturbance, muscle tremor, and movement disorders. MeHg exposures are associated with cognitive declines in children exposed prenatally and postnatally.

TABLE A.2 Additional information and detailed profiles on methylmercury

SOURCE	DESCRIPTION
Committee on the Toxicological Effects of Methylmercury, Board on Environmental Studies and Toxicology, Commission on Life Sciences, and National Research Council. 2000. *Toxicological Effects of Methylmercury.* Washington, DC: National Academies Press.	Reviews health effects of MeHg; discusses the estimation of mercury exposure from measured biomarkers; appropriate statistical methods for data analysis and reviews available epidemiological studies
ATSDR (US Agency for Toxic Substances and Disease Registry). 1999. "Toxicological Profile for Mercury." Atlanta: ATSDR.	Link to ATSDR toxicological profiles, as well as community resources and other resources for health professionals
IPCS (International Programme on Chemical Safety). 1990. "Environmental Health Criteria 101, Methylmercury." EHC document. Geneva: IPCS, World Health Organization, and United Nations Environment Programme.	Reviews data and risks to human health from compounds of MeHg
WHO, UNEP, and IOMC (World Health Organization, United Nations Environment Programme, and Inter-Organization Programme for the Sound Management of Chemicals). 2008. "Guidance for Identifying Populations at Risk from Mercury Exposure." Guide and reference document. Geneva: WHO and UNEP.	Includes guidelines and numerous resources (food frequency questionnaire, cognitive testing) focusing on MeHg

Source: World Bank compilation.

LEAD (Pb)

Sources

Lead occurs naturally in the environment in ores and has many uses, including automobile batteries, leaded gasoline (at one time), lead alloys, use in soldering materials, shielding for x-ray machines, in the manufacture of corrosion-resistant and acid-resistant materials used in the building industry, and a variety of dyes and pigments. Prior to World War II, Pb was used extensively in pesticides. The amount of Pb contained in pipes and plumbing fittings has decreased substantially, but many areas still have public water-distribution systems containing Pb. Other sources of Pb exposure include lead glazing on pottery. Pb has also been found as an additive to nonpharmaceutical health remedies and spices.

Health outcomes

The primary health outcome associated with exposure to Pb is cognitive deficits in children exposed prenatally and throughout childhood.

Pb alters the hematological system by inhibiting the activities of several enzymes involved in heme biosynthesis, particularly δ-aminolevulinic acid dehydratase (ALAD), leading to clinical anemia. Population studies suggest an association between bone-lead levels (measured by XRF) and elevated blood pressure, which may lead to other cardiovascular-health outcomes. Pb is also associated with renal effects, including kidney function, such as glomerular-filtration rate.

TABLE A.3 **Additional information and detailed profiles on lead**

SOURCE	DESCRIPTION
ATSDR (US Agency for Toxic Substances and Disease Registry). 2020. "Toxicological Profile for Lead." Atlanta: ATSDR.	Toxicological profile, community information, environmental health and medical education; many resources for health professionals
Health Canada. 2013. *Final Human Health State of the Science Report on Lead.* Ottawa: Health Canada.	Toxicological profile, Canadian regulatory perspective
IPCS (International Programme on Chemical Safety). 1995. "Inorganic Lead. Environmental Health Criteria 165." EHC document. Geneva: IPCS, World Health Organization, and United Nations Environment Programme.	Detailed toxicological profile
Nawrot, T. S., L. Thijs, E. M. Den Hond, H. A. Roels, and J. A. Staessen. 2002. "An Epidemiological Re-Appraisal of the Association between Blood Pressure and Blood Lead: A Meta-Analysis." *Journal of Human Hypertension* 16: 123–31.	Meta-analysis of potential cardiovascular effects

Source: World Bank compilation.

ARSENIC (As); INORGANIC As (iAs)

Sources

Arsenic in its inorganic form occurs naturally in soil and water worldwide and is found in many different types of ore. As is mobilized and released through a variety of human activities, including smelting, use of arsenic-based pesticides, and many other industrial processes. As also occurs naturally in groundwater in many parts of the world, and people can be exposed from naturally occurring As through household use of this water, including drinking, bathing, cooking, and other activities. Naturally occurring As is also used as irrigation water in many parts of the world, particularly for rice, and is therefore measurable in most rice products, especially those from Southeast Asia.

Health outcomes

Exposures to arsenic have been associated with a variety of health outcomes affecting virtually every organ system in the human body. Among the most obvious clinical symptoms are skin rashes and lesions such as hyperkeratosis and hyperpigmentation, which may lead to skin cancer. Often these rashes begin on the hands and extremities, and a noted delayed effect of acute or chronic exposure may be seen as Mee's lines in nails (for example, horizontal lines). As is a known human carcinogen, with the strongest association seen with skin cancer, followed by bladder and lung cancer. Arsenic is also associated with neurotoxic and neurodevelopmental outcomes, including cognitive deficits in children and peripheral neuropathy. A variety of other health outcomes has been reported, ranging from gastrointestinal to cardiovascular effects. Reported cardiac effects include altered myocardial depolarization (prolonged QT interval and nonspecific ST-segment changes), cardiac arrhythmias, and ischemic heart disease.

TABLE A.4 **Additional information and detailed profiles on arsenic**

SOURCE	DESCRIPTION
ATSDR (US Agency for Toxic Substances and Disease Registry). 2007. "Toxicological Profile for Arsenic." Atlanta: ATSDR.	Toxicological profile, community information, environmental health and medical education; many resources for health professionals
WHO (World Health Organization). 1981. Arsenic (Environmental Health Criteria 18). Geneva: WHO. file:///C:/Users/16507/Desktop/Downloads/9241540788-eng.pdf.	Detailed toxicological profile
EA (Environment Agency). 2009. "Soil Guideline Values for Inorganic Arsenic in Soil." Science Report SC050021/arsenic SGV. Bristol, UK: EA.	Contains toxicological information; describes environmental fate and exposure pathways
A. Gomez-Caminero, P. Howe, M. Hughes, E. Kenyon, D. R. Lewis, M. Moore, J. Ng, A. Aitio, and G. Becking. 2001. *Environmental Health Criteria 224: Arsenic and Arsenic Compounds.* Geneva: World Health Organization.	Data and review to establish the scientific basis for risk assessment of As
NTP (National Toxicology Program). 2016. "Arsenic and Inorganic Arsenic Compounds." In *Report on Carcinogens*, 14th ed. Washington, DC: US Department of Health and Human Services.	US-based assessment of carcinogenicity of As

Source: World Bank compilation.

Guidelines for Designing and Conducting Home Surveys

A home survey questionnaire will be used to obtain information on relevant demographics, housing characteristics, behaviors, activity patterns, intake rates, other site- or population-specific exposure factors, and basic health information from participants at artisanal, small-scale gold-mining (ASGM) sites. This appendix provides general guidelines for the types of questions that should be included in the household survey and recommended response categories. Important factors that will need to be considered on a site-by-site basis are also noted. The final (formatted) survey questionnaire to be administered in the field should be developed by the in-field research team based on the resources provided here. It is recommended that the questionnaire responses be entered into a portable computer in real time, if possible, to avoid hard-copy losses or subsequent data-entry errors and to facilitate the data-analysis process. It is essential that the household survey be administered to the same individual household members for whom the environmental (chapter 3), biomonitoring (chapter 4), and health-outcome (chapter 5) data are collected. The same home survey instrument should be administered to households in both the identified ASGM sites and matched control sites. Note that any necessary ethical clearances will need to be obtained prior to sample collection by the in-field research team.

WHO, UNEP, and IOMC (World Health Organization, United Nations Environment Programme, and Inter-Organization Programme for the Sound Management of Chemicals). 2008. "Guidance for Identifying Populations at Risk from Mercury Exposure." Reference document. Geneva: WHO and UNEP. https://www.who.int/foodsafety/publications/chem /mercuryexposure.pdf.

This reference is a key resource for identifying populations potentially at risk from exposure to mercury (Hg) and methylmercury (MeHg). It provides specific examples of socioeconomic and health-outcome survey instruments specific to Hg and MeHg exposures.

GUIDANCE FOR POWER CALCULATIONS, OPTIMAL SAMPLE SIZES, AND HEALTH SURVEY DESIGN

Aday, L. A., and L. J. Cornelius. 2006. *Designing and Conducting Health Surveys: A Comprehensive Guide,* 3rd ed. San Francisco: Jossey-Bass, an imprint of John Wiley & Sons.

This reference is a key resource for designing and conducting health surveys, providing details for designing health surveys using high-quality, effective, and efficient statistical and methodological practices as well as providing optimal sample designs. It is also important that subsequent applications of estimation strategies to the survey data, as well as analytical techniques and interpretations of resultant research findings, are guided by well-grounded statistical theory, and this reference provides these details.

Adcock, C. J. 1997. "Sample Size Determination: A Review." Journal of the Royal Statistical Society: Series D (The Statistician) 46 (2): 261–83.

This article provides a review of estimating appropriate sample sizes using both frequentist and Bayesian methods.

Greenland, S. 1993. "Methods for Epidemiologic Analyses of Multiple Exposures: A Review and Comparative Study of Maximum-Likelihood, Preliminary-Testing, and Empirical-Bayes Regression." Statistics in Medicine 12 (8): 717–36.

Many epidemiologic investigations are designed to study the effects of multiple exposures. Most of these studies are analyzed either by fitting a risk-regression model with all exposures forced in the model, or by using a preliminary-testing algorithm, such as stepwise regression, to produce a smaller model. Research indicates that hierarchical-modeling methods can outperform these conventional approaches, as discussed in this review.

Lubin, J. H., M. H. Gail, and A. G. Ershow. 1988. "Sample Size and Power for Case-Control Studies When Exposures Are Continuous." *Statistics in Medicine* 7 (3): 363–76.

Environmental exposures are continuous, and dichotomization may result in a "not exposed" category that has little practical meaning. In addition, if risks vary monotonically with exposure, then dichotomization will obscure risk effects and require a greater number of subjects to detect differences in the exposure distributions among cases and referents. Starting from the usual score statistic to detect differences in exposure, this paper develops sample-size formulae for case-control studies with arbitrary exposure distributions; this includes both continuous and dichotomous exposure measurements as special cases.

Lui, K.-J. 1993. "Sample Size Determination for Multiple Continuous Risk Factors in Case-Control Studies." *Biometrics* 49 (3): 873–76.

For a desired power of detecting the association between a disease and several potential risk factors in case-control studies, it is difficult to choose appropriate values for each parameter in the alternative hypothesis. A proposed statistical strategy is discussed.

Lwanga, S. K., and S. Lemeshow. 1991. *Sample Size Determination in Health Studies: A Practical Manual.* Geneva: World Health Organization.

This manual provides the practical and statistical information needed to help investigators decide how large a sample to select from a population targeted for a health study or survey. Designed to perform a "cookbook function," the book uses explanatory text and abundant tabular calculations to vastly simplify the task of determining the minimum sample size needed to obtain statistically valid results given a set of simple hypotheses.

Thomas, D. C., J. Siemiatycki, R. Dewar, J. Robins, M. Goldberg, and B. G. Armstrong. 1985. "The Problem of Multiple Inference in Studies Designed to Generate Hypotheses." *American Journal of Epidemiology* 122 (6): 1080–95.

Epidemiologic research often involves the simultaneous assessment of associations between many risk factors and several disease outcomes. In such situations, often designed to generate hypotheses, multiple univariate hypothesis testing is not an appropriate basis for inference. This paper discusses an approach in which all associations in the data are reported, whether significant or not, followed by a ranking in order of priority for investigation using empirical Bayesian techniques.

EXPOSURE HISTORY RESOURCES

The US Agency for Toxic Substances and Disease Registry (ATSDR) provides educational and resource materials for taking exposure histories in adults and children, and shows how this information can be linked to potential health outcomes.

ANNOTATED REFERENCES ON FOOD FREQUENCY QUESTIONNAIRES

Several food-frequency questionnaire (FFQ) templates are available to use as guides for developing a specific FFQ in the context of exposures in low- and middle-income countries (LMICs). For the research proposed here, an important aspect of the FFQ is to identify the amount and frequency of consumption of locally produced agricultural products and locally caught fish and shellfish that may be affected by contaminants of concern (CoCs) originating from ASGM activities.

The US National Cancer Institute (US NCI) has developed guidance on FFQs to support assessments of dietary and nutritional supplement intake.

The Women's Health Initiative (WHI) is a long-term national health study with both observational and clinical components involving over 40 health centers. The original WHI study included 161,808 postmenopausal women enrolled between 1993 and 1998. The Fred Hutchinson Cancer Research Center in Seattle serves as the WHI Clinical Coordinating Center for data collection, management, and analysis of the WHI. One aspect of the WHI involves application of a detailed dietary assessment, including several food-frequency questionnaires.

WHO, UNEP, and IOMC (World Health Organization, United Nations Environment Programme, and Inter-Organization Programme for the Sound Management of Chemicals). 2008. "Guidance for Identifying Populations at Risk from Mercury Exposure." Reference document. Geneva: WHO and UNEP. https://www.who.int/foodsafety/publications/chem /mercuryexposure.pdf.

This publication contains examples of an FFQ, health-assessment questionnaire, and socioeconomic questionnaire, as well as sample collection guidelines for urine, blood, and hair.

ADDITIONAL FFQ REFERENCES:

Boynton, P. M., and T. Greenhalgh. "Hands-On Guide to Questionnaire Research: Selecting, Designing, and Developing Your Questionnaire." *BMJ* 328 (7451): 1312–15.

Cade, J., R. Thompson, V. Burley, and D. Warm. 2002. "Development, Validation and Utilisation of Food-Frequency Questionnaires: A Review." *Public Health Nutrition* 5 (4): 567–87.

Matthys, C., I. Pynaert, W. De Keyzer, and S. De Henauw. 2007. "Validity and Reproducibility of an Adolescent Web-Based Food Frequency Questionnaire." *Journal of the American Dietetic Association* 107 (4): 605–10.

Shim, J.-S., K. Oh, and H. C. Kim. 2014. "Dietary Assessment Methods in Epidemiologic Studies." *Epidemiology and Health* 36: e2014009.

ADDITIONAL LMIC-SPECIFIC RESOURCES

Population-based surveys, repeated approximately every five years, are now available for more than 100 LMICs, providing information on nutritional status, health-related behaviors, morbidity, and mortality. These include Demographic and Health Surveys under the auspices of the US Agency for International Development (USAID) and Multiple Indicator Cluster Surveys conducted by the United Nations Children's Fund (UNICEF).

SAMPLE HOME SURVEY QUESTIONNAIRE

Each survey question should have a predetermined list of responses (that is, check-box categories) to ensure uniformity in response options across participants. Open-ended questions should generally be avoided. Note that an adult will need to provide the answer for some (or all) questions on behalf of sampled children.

1. Demographics (provide information on age, sex, length of residence, education, income, household size, and composition)
    1.1   How old are you? (check box for category of age ranges; for example, 6–10 years, 11–15 years)
    1.2   What is your gender identity? (check box)
    1.3   How long have you lived here? (check box for date ranges; for example, 1–2 years, 3–5 years)
    1.4   Where did you live previously? (used to determine whether previous residence was in a similar exposure zone) (*need to determine list of possible neighborhoods, cities, regions in advance)
    1.5   How long did you live there? (check box for date ranges; for example, 1–2 years, 3–5 years)
    1.6   What is your highest level of education? (check box for education ranges; for example, grade school, secondary school)
    1.7   What is your income level? (check box for income ranges) (*need to determine appropriate ranges and $ units in advance)

1.8 What is the size of your current household? (check box for household ranges; for example, 1–2 people, 3–4 people)

1.9 Who (and how many) are the other family members? (check all that apply; for example, brother [#], sister [#], mother, father, grandmother)

2. Occupation/School (seeking information on possible workplace, off-site, or take-home exposures)

2.1 Do you work or attend school outside the home? [if y → 2.2; if n → 3]

2.2 What do you do? (*need to determine possible industry sectors or schools in advance)

2.3 Where is that located? (*need to identify possible zone or sector relative to exposure source in advance; map-based)

2.4 How long have you worked / attended school there? (check box for date ranges)

2.5 How much time do you spend at your occupation?

2.6 Do you work with or handle chemicals in any way? [If y → 2.6a; if n → 2.7] (define "chemicals" in advance)

2.6a What chemicals do you work with or handle? (*need to identify possible list of chemicals or materials/products that contain chemicals in advance)

2.6b Do you wear protective equipment (PPE)? (*need to define PPE and give list of options; for example, gloves, clothing, dust mask, respirator)

2.6c Do you get any of the chemicals on your skin, hair, or clothing?

2.6d Do you wash off before coming home?

2.6e Do you wash off when you get home or remove clothes?

2.6f Who washes clothing? (check box for possible options; for example, self, spouse, child)

2.6g Where are clothes washed? (*need to identify possible option in advance)

2.7 If attend school, do you play outdoors or in soil? (check box for either/both) [if y → 2.7a; if n → 3.0]

2.7a How often? (check box for frequency ranges; for example, 1–2 days per week, 3–4 days per week)

2.7b How long? (check box for duration ranges; for example, 0.5–1 hour/day, 2–3 hours/day)

3. Time-Activity Patterns and Lifestyle/Housing Characteristics (seeking information on exposure factors and lifestyle/housing details, including other possible sources of exposure)

3.1 Is there a wood-burning stove and/or fireplace in the home? [if y → 3.1a if n → 3.2]

3.1a What type of wood (or other material) is burned?

3.1b How often?

3.1c Where (for example, kitchen)?

3.2 How close is the home to the road/traffic? (check box for distance ranges; for example, 10–100 yards)

3.3 What kind of traffic (car, bike, horse, foot)? Is the road dusty?

3.4 Do you use pesticides or chemicals inside or outside the home (for example, pest control, gardening, and so forth)? [if y → 3.4.a; if n → 3.5]

3.4a What kinds of chemicals/pesticides do you use? (checkoff list)

3.4b How much do you use? (quantity choices)

3.5 How much time do you spend

- Outside the home (for example, work, school, other activities) (check boxes for time spent at each location; for example, 0.5–1 hour/day) (*Need questions re: whether [how often/how long] spend time playing in soil at home [yard, garden] or other locations)
- Inside the home (approximate time in areas of the home [for example, communal space, kitchen, sleeping, and so forth])

Do you have a dirt floor? [if y → 3.5.a; if n → 3.6]

3.5a How do you (or other family member) clean the floor? (check all cleaning options that apply; for example, sweeping, mopping—may need to identify options in advance)

3.5b How often do you (or other family member) clean the floor? (check box for frequency options; for example, 1–2 times per week, 3–4 times per week)

3.6 What is the floor material? (*need to identify possible materials in advance)

3.7 What is the building material of the home? (*need to identify possible materials in advance)

3.8 What type of roof? (*need to identify possible materials in advance)

3.9 Are there windows? How many? Which rooms? Covered or open? (some findings may be based on personal observations while administering survey)

3.10 How many doors? What material? Gaps around door frame? (some findings may be based on personal observations while administering survey)

3.11 What is ventilation/air exchange like in the home? (*need to identify possible descriptors in advance; may also be based on personal observations)

3.12 Is the home dusty? (questions plus observation) How often cleaned? How cleaned?

3.13 How many floors is home (single versus multistory)?
How is house arranged—bedrooms, kitchen, living area, and so forth (draw map?)

3.14 Do any animals stay inside home? What kind? How many? Where? Contact with household members?

3.15 Do you wear shoes? Track dirt in home?

3.16 Ask questions related to frequency and duration of hand-to-mouth and object-to-mouth activities

3.17 Ask questions related to showering/bathing—where done? Source of water? Frequency and duration?

3.18 Ask questions related to aluminum cookware (contains lead)

4. Health Status (seeking information on current health and possible comorbidities; note that this chapter may be superseded in the event of a more formal medical examination—see chapter 4)

4.1 Do you have any diagnosed chronic illnesses? (diabetes, cancer, list and check off with a write-in option?)

4.2 Do you have any acute or chronic health issues? (for example, persistent cough, tremors, skin rashes, and so forth; develop a master list and check off symptoms as appropriate)

4.3 Do you smoke? [If y → 4.3a; if n → 4.4]

4.3a How many cigarettes (or cigars?) do you smoke in a day?

4.3b How long have you been smoking (for example, years)?

4.3c What brand cigarettes? Filtered or unfiltered?

4.4 Do you drink alcohol? [if y → 4.4.a; if n → 4.5]

4.4a How much alcohol do you drink in a typical week?

4.5 Are you physically active?

4.6 Height (cm)

4.7 Weight (kg)

4.8 Body mass index (BMI; calculated)

4.9 Ask questions related to malaria, dengue fever, diarrhea, or other region-specific infectious or other issues

4.10 Ask questions (here or below) that get at nutritional or vitamin-deficiency issues

4.11 Use of traditional medicines (contain metals)

Unique to ASGM–chronic inorganic mercury intoxication (CIMI) neurological checklist:

4.12 Do you work at any ASGM-related activities?

4.13 Do you work with mercury or with mercury-polluted tailings?

4.14 Do you burn amalgam in the open?

4.15 Do you melt gold in the open or with inadequate fume hoods?

4.16 Do you ever experience a metallic taste in your mouth?

4.17 Do you ever have excessive salivation?

4.18 Do you have tremors or do your hands shake?

4.19 Do you have trouble falling or staying asleep?

5. Dietary Information (seeking information on intake rates)

5.1 In general, how would you describe your diet?

5.2 Do you eat vegetables/meat/dairy from your own or nearby gardens?

5.3 Have you eaten seafood in the last 72 hours (important for biomonitoring of As)

5.4 How much water do you drink in a day? (liters)

5.5 Where does your water come from? (location, well, tap)

5.6 Questions related to local fishing, such as types of fish, and so forth

5.7 Food Frequency Questionnaire (FQQ)

6. Cost of Illness Economics-Related Information (all questions are based on the previous year)

6.1 How many days during the last year have you missed work because of illness?

6.2 How much income did you lose in the last year because of illness?

6.3 How many times did you visit the emergency room or health center?

6.4 How many nights did you spend in a hospital or health center?

6.5 How much did you spend on health care in the last year?

APPENDIX C

Key References and Resource Guides for Environmental Sampling

GUIDELINES FOR SITE CHARACTERIZATION AND DEVELOPING SAMPLING PLANS

When developing a site-specific characterization and sampling plan, multiple resources are available for consultation, as listed and described in table C.1.

TABLE C.1 **Site-characterization resources**

SOURCE	DESCRIPTION
Canadian Council of Ministers of the Environment. *Guidance Manual for Environmental Site Characterization in Support of Environmental and Human Health Risk Assessment.* https://ccme.ca/en/res /guidancemanual-environmentalsitecharacterization_vol _1e.pdf	Guidance for site characterization, risk assessment, and general contaminated-site assessment
Demetriades, A., and M. Birke. 2015. *Urban Geochemical Mapping Manual: Sampling, Sample Preparation, Laboratory Analysis, Quality Control Check, Statistical Processing and Map Plotting.* Brussels: EuroGeoSurveys.	Guidelines provided by EuroGeoSurveys out of Brussels; provides detailed information on mapping and site characterization from a European perspective
ESDAC (European Soil Data Centre) website: https://esdac .jrc.ec.europa.eu/.	The European Soil Data Centre (ESDAC) of the European Commission's Joint Research Centre is the thematic center for soil-related data in Europe. The goal is to be the single reference point for and to host all relevant soil data and information at the European level. It contains a number of resources: datasets, services or applications, maps, documents, events, projects, and external links.
EPA (US Environmental Protection Agency). 1989. "Interim Final RCRA Facility Investigation (RFI) Guidance, Volume II of IV: Soil, Ground Water and Subsurface Gas Releases." EPA 530/SW-89-031. Washington, DC: EPA.	Provides guidance on site characterization and sampling strategies
EPA (US Environmental Protection Agency). 2014. "Sampling and Analysis Plan—Guidance and Template: Version 4, General Projects." R9QA/009.1. Washington, DC: EPA.	This Sampling and Analysis Plan (SAP) guidance and template is intended to assist organizations in documenting procedural and analytical requirements for projects involving the collection of water, soil, sediment, or other samples taken to characterize areas of potential environmental contamination.

continued

TABLE C.1, *continued*

SOURCE	DESCRIPTION
ISO (International Organization for Standardization). 2017. ISO 18400-105:2017, Soil quality—Sampling—Part 105: Packaging, transport, storage and preservation of samples.	Establishes general principles for packing, preservation, transport, and delivery of soil samples and related materials; requirements for chemical analysis of samples
Olusola, O. I., and O. K. Aisha. 2007. "Towards Standardization of Sampling Methodology for Evaluation of Soil Pollution in Nigeria." *Journal of Applied Sciences and Environmental Management* 11 (3): 81–85.	"Proposes…procedure…for comparable, representative and cost effective, soil sampling; …explores…policy issues regarding standardization of sampling activities and analytical process as it relates to soil pollution in Nigeria" (Olusola and Aisha 2007, 81).

Source: World Bank compilation.

TABLE C.2 Criteria for analytical-method selection

CRITERIA[a]	RATIONALE
Gold standard	Method demonstrates contaminant and matrix specificity; widely used in epidemiological studies
Broadly applicable	Applies to more than just one contaminant
Used in LMIC studies	Documented use in the literature
Feasibility	In field versus send to lab and correlation between field and laboratory results
Cost	To be determined
Detection level	Detection level relative to expected concentrations
Capability	Laboratory likely to have calibrated method
Local capability	In consultation with local expertise

Source: World Bank.
Note: a. Criteria given in order of importance. LMIC = low- to middle-income country.

LABORATORY METHODS FOR ENVIRONMENTAL SAMPLING

The US-based ASTM International (https://www.astm.org/) (formerly known as the American Society for Testing and Materials) and the International Standards Organization (ISO, https://www.iso.org/) are the preeminent organizations providing guidelines and standards for collecting and analyzing environmental samples across different matrices. The specific methods chosen to analyze metals in water, soil, dust, agricultural products, fish, and other matrices—such as sludge, fertilizer, and solid wastes—will depend on many factors, some of which can be determined *a priori* and some of which will require additional collaboration by the accredited laboratory performing the analyses and the in-field research team. The general criteria for method evaluation are given in table C.2.

Table C.3 provides a nonexhaustive list of resources most often used internationally in selecting analytical methods for contaminated-site assessments. Relevant US Environmental Protection Agency (EPA) laboratory methods for environmental sampling are shown in table C.4.

TABLE C.3 Sources of analytical guidelines for contaminated-site assessments

SOURCE	DESCRIPTION
ASTM International website: https://www.astm.org/	Internationally recognized as the authority on guidance and guidelines for laboratory testing, collecting samples, metals analysis, and many other standards. Available for purchase individually or by subscription by topic.
Cordeiro, F., S. Gonçalves, J. Calderón, P. Robouch, H. Emteborg, P. Conneely, M.-F. Tumba-Tshilumba, B. Kortsen, and B. de la Calle. 2013. *IMEP-115: Determination of Methylmercury in Seafood.* Luxembourg: European Union.	Related to the citation above (https://www.astm.org/); focuses on MeHg in seafood. Recommended method. Supports Commission Regulations 1881/2006 and 882/2004.
EA (Environment Agency). 2006. "The Determination of Metals in Solid Environmental Samples: Methods for the Examination of Waters and Associated Materials." Booklet. Bristol, UK: EA.	Guidance from the UK Environment Agency on laboratory methods for metals in solid matrices.
EPA (US Environmental Protection Agency). n.d. "Collection of Methods." Environment Measurements and Modeling, EPA website: https://www.epa.gov/measurements-modeling/collection-methods.	EPA offices and laboratories, and outside organizations, have developed approved methods for measuring contaminant concentrations. Contains extensive links to many laboratory resources and a complete listing of approved methods.
EPA (US Environmental Protection Agency). n.d. "The SW-486 Compendium." https://www.epa.gov/hw-sw846/sw-846-compendium.	US EPA's SW-846 Compendium provides a complete listing and guidance of all US EPA-approved laboratory methods. Most methods are intended as guidance.
European Union Reference Laboratory for Heavy Metals in Feed and Food (EURL-HM), European Commission. https://www.feedsafety.org/activities/eurl/eurl-heavy-metals/	Determination of As, Cd, Hg, and Pb in food and feed products including pet food; validated a method for the determination of MeHg in seafood; determination of iAs in food of vegetable origin.
Euro Chlor. 2009. *Determination of Mercury in Liquids: Analytical 7, 3rd Edition.* Reference manual. Brussels: Euro Chlor.	Discussion of cold-vapor atomic absorption spectrometry (CVAAS) and cold vapor atomic fluorescence spectrometry (CVAFS) for measuring Hg in water.
Hageman, P. L. 2007. "Determination of Mercury in Aqueous and Geologic Materials by Continuous Flow–Cold Vapor–Atomic Fluorescence Spectrometry (CVAFS)." In *U.S. Geological Survey Techniques and Methods*, Book 5, Chapter 2. Reston, VA: United States Geological Survey.	Discussion of updated CVAAS methods for determining total Hg in geologic materials and dissolved Hg in aqueous samples; replaces the methods in use prior to 2006.
ISO (International Organization for Standardization). 2013. ISO 16729:2013, Soil quality—Digestion of nitric acid soluble fractions of elements.	Microwave digestion of sludge, treated biowaste, and soil using nitric acid suitable for all metals.
ISO (International Organization for Standardization). 2013. ISO/TS 16965:2013, Soil quality—Determination of trace elements using inductively coupled plasma mass spectrometry (ICP-MS).	Specifies a method for determining metals in aqua regia or nitric acid digests or other extraction solutions of sludge, treated biowaste, and soil.
ISO (International Organization for Standardization). 2012. ISO 12846:2012, Water quality—Determination of mercury—Method using atomic absorption spectrometry (AAS) with and without enrichment.	Specifies two methods for determining Hg in drinking, surface, ground, rain, and wastewater after appropriate predigestion.
ISO (International Organization for Standardization). 2004. ISO 16772:2004, Soil quality—Determination of mercury in aqua regia soil extracts with cold-vapour atomic spectrometry or cold-vapour atomic fluorescence spectrometry.	Specifies a method for determining Hg in an aqua regia extract of soil using cold-vapor atomic-absorption spectrometry or cold-vapor atomic-fluorescence spectrometry.
ISO (International Organization for Standardization). 2013. ISO/TS 16727:2013, Soil quality—Determination of mercury—Cold vapour atomic fluorescence spectrometry (CVAFS).	Specifies a method for determining Hg in aqua regia or nitric acid digests of sludge, treated biowaste, and soil using cold-vapor atomic-fluorescence spectrometry.

continued

TABLE C.3, *continued*

SOURCE	DESCRIPTION
Lasorsa, B. K., G. A. Gill, and M. Horvat. 2012. "Analytical Methods for Measuring Mercury in Water, Sediment, and Biota." In *Mercury in the Environment: Pattern and Process*, edited by M. S. Bank, 27–54. Berkeley: University of California Press. doi:10.1525 /california/9780520271630.003.0003	Discussion of analytical techniques for understanding Hg chemistry in natural systems; determination of total and major species of Hg in water, sediments and soils, and biota. Guidance for analytical methods that can be utilized, depending on the nature of the sample, detection levels, and what species or fraction is to be quantified.
Ministry of the Environment, Japan. 2004. "Mercury Analysis Manual." Ministry of the Environment. Tokyo: Government of Japan.	Extensive discussion of internationally accepted analytical methods for Hg and MeHg.
USGS (United States Geological Survey). "Methods Compilation," USGS Mercury Research Laboratory, last modified September 26, 2017, https://wi.water.usgs.gov/mercury-lab/research/analysis -methods.html.	Complete and detailed links to Hg and MeHg analysis methods referencing specific instruments.

Source: World Bank compilation.

TABLE C.4 US EPA laboratory methods

METHOD #	TITLE	TYPE	ANALYTE	TECHNIQUE	MEDIA/MATRIX	DATE
3005A	Acid Digestion of Waters for Total Recoverable or Dissolved Metals for Analysis by FLAA or ICP Spectroscopy. https://www .epa.gov/sites/default/files/2015 -12/documents/3005a.pdf	Sample preparation	Multi-metal screen; As, Pb	Acid digestion	Surface water, groundwater	July 1992
3010A	Acid Digestion of Aqueous Samples and Extracts for Total Metals for Analysis by FLAA or ICP Spectroscopy. https://www .epa.gov/sites/default/files/2015 -12/documents/3010a.pdf	Sample preparation	Multi-metal screen; As, Pb	Acid digestion	Aqueous samples, extracts, wastes with suspended solids	July 1992
3015A	Microwave Assisted Acid Digestion of Aqueous Samples and Extracts. https://www.epa .gov/sites/default/files/2015-12 /documents/3015a.pdf	Sample preparation	Multi-metal screen; As, Pb	Microwave-assisted acid digestion	Aqueous samples, drinking water, extracts, wastes with suspended solids	Feb. 2007
3020A	Acid Digestion of Aqueous Samples and Extracts for Total Metals for Analysis by GFAA Spectroscopy. https://www.epa .gov/hw-sw846/sw-846-test -method-3020a-acid-digestion -aqueous-samples-and-extracts -total-metals-analysis	Sample preparation	Pb	Acid digestion	Aqueous samples, extracts, wastes with suspended solids	July 1992
3031	Acid Digestion of Oils for Metals Analysis by Atomic Absorption or ICP Spectrometry. https://19january2017snapshot .epa.gov/sites/production/files /2015-07/documents/epa-3031 .pdf	Sample preparation	Multi-metal screen; As, Pb	Acid digestion	Oils, oil sludges, tars, waxes, paints, paint sludges, other viscous petroleum products	Dec. 1996

continued

TABLE C.4, *continued*

METHOD #	TITLE	TYPE	ANALYTE	TECHNIQUE	MEDIA/MATRIX	DATE
3040A	Dissolution Procedure for Oils, Greases, or Waxes. https://www .epa.gov/sites/default/files/2015 -12/documents/3040a.pdf	Sample preparation	Multi-metal screen; As, Pb	Solvent dissolution	Oils, greases, waxes	Dec. 1996
3050B	Acid Digestion of Sediments, Sludges, and Soils. https://www .epa.gov/sites/default/files/2015 -06/documents/epa-3050b.pdf	Sample preparation	Multi-metal screen; As, Pb	Acid digestion	Sediments, sludges, soils, and oils	Dec. 1996
3051A	Microwave Assisted Acid Digestion of Sediments, Sludges, Soils, and Oils. https:// www.epa.gov/sites/default/files /2015-06/documents/epa-3050b .pdf	Sample preparation	Multi-metal screen; As, Pb	Microwave-assisted acid digestion	Sediments, sludges, soils, and oils	Feb. 2007
7010	Graphite Furnace Atomic Absorption Spectrophotometry. https://www.epa.gov/sites /default/files/2015-07 /documents/epa-7010.pdf	Determinative	Multi-metal screen; As, Pb	Graphite furnace atomic absorption spectrophotometry (GFAA or GFAAS)	Groundwater, domestic wastes, industrial wastes, extracts, soils, sludges, sediments	Feb. 2007
7000B	Flame Atomic Absorption Spectrophotometry. https:// www.epa.gov/sites/default/files /2015-12/documents/7000b.pdf	Determinative	Pb	Flame atomic absorption spectrophotometry (FLAA or FAAS)	Groundwater, aqueous samples, extracts, industrial waste, soils, sludges, sediments	Feb. 2007
6800	Elemental and Molecular Speciated Isotope Dilution Mass Spectrometry. https://www.epa .gov/sites/default/files/2015-12 /documents/6800.pdf	Determinative	Pb	Isotope dilution mass spectrometry (IDMS), molecular speciated isotope dilution mass spectrometry (SIDMS)	Water samples, solid samples, extracts, digests, blood, foods	July 2014
6200	Field Portable X-Ray Fluorescence Spectrometry for the Determination of Elemental Concentrations in Soil and Sediment. https://www.epa.gov /hw-sw846/sw-846-test-method -6200-field-portable-x-ray -fluorescence-spectrometry -determination	Determinative	Multi-metal screen; As, Pb	X-ray fluorescence	Soils, sediment	Feb. 2007
6020B	Inductively Coupled Plasma- Mass Spectrometry. https:// www.epa.gov/sites/default/files /2015-12/documents/6020b.pdf	Determinative	Multi-metal screen; As, Pb	Inductively coupled plasma–mass spectrometry (ICP-MS)	Water samples, waste extracts, digests	July 2014

continued

TABLE C.4, *continued*

METHOD #	TITLE	TYPE	ANALYTE	TECHNIQUE	MEDIA/MATRIX	DATE
6010D	Inductively Coupled Plasma-Optical Emissions Spectrometry. https://www.epa.gov/hw-sw846/sw-846-test-method-6010d-inductively-coupled-plasma-optical-emission-spectrometry-icp-oes	Determinative	Multi-metal screen; As, Pb	Inductively coupled plasma-atomic (or optical) emission spectrometry (ICP-AES or ICP-OES)	Groundwater, digested aqueous and solid matrices	July 2014
3052	Microwave Assisted Acid Digestion of Siliceous and Organically Based Matrices. https://19january2017snapshot.epa.gov/hw-sw846/sw-846-test-method-3052-microwave-assisted-acid-digestion-siliceous-and-organically-based_.html	Sample preparation	Multi-metal screen; As, Pb	Microwave-assisted acid digestion	Siliceous matrices, organic matrices, and other complex matrices	Dec. 1996
7472	Mercury in Aqueous Samples and Extracts by Anodic Stripping Voltammetry (ASV). https://www.epa.gov/sites/default/files/2015-12/documents/7472.pdf	Determinative	Hg	Anodic stripping voltammetry (ASV)	Drinking water, natural surface water, seawater, domestic or industrial wastewater, soil extracts	Dec. 1996
7473	Mercury in Solids and Solutions by Thermal Decomposition, Amalgamation, and Atomic Absorption Spectrophotometry. https://www.epa.gov/hw-sw846/sw-846-test-method-7473-mercury-solids-and-solutions-thermal-decomposition-amalgamation-and	Determinative	Hg	Thermal decomposition and atomic absorption spectrophotometry (AAS)	Solids, aqueous samples, digested solutions	Feb. 2007
7474	Mercury in Sediment and Tissue Samples by Atomic Fluorescence Spectrometry. https://www.epa.gov/hw-sw846/sw-846-test-method-7474-mercury-sediment-and-tissue-samples-atomic-fluorescence	Determinative	Hg	Atomic fluorescence spectrometry (AFS)	Sediment, tissue	Feb. 2007

Source: World Bank compilation.
Note: As = arsenic; EPA = US Environmental Protection Agency; FLAA = lead analysis by flame atomic absorption; GFAA = graphite furnace atomic absorption spectroscopy; Hg = mercury; ICP = inductively coupled plasma analysis; Pb = lead.

BIOACCESSIBILITY AND BIOAVAILABILITY OF LEAD AND ARSENIC: US EPA GUIDANCE

EPA (US Environmental Protection Agency). 2007. "Guidance for Evaluating the Oral Bioavailability of Metals in Soils for Use in Human Health Risk Assessment." OSWER 9285.7-80. Washington, DC: EPA.

EPA (US Environmental Protection Agency). 2015. "Guidance for Sample Collection for *In Vitro* Bioaccessibility Assay for Lead (Pb) in Soil." OSWER 9200.3-100. Washington, DC: EPA.

EPA (US Environmental Protection Agency). 2017. "Method 1340: *In Vitro* Bioaccessibility Assay for Lead in Soil." SW-846 Update VI. Washington, DC: EPA.

EPA (US Environmental Protection Agency). 2017. "Release of Standard Operating Procedure for an In Vitro Bioaccessibility Assay for Lead and Arsenic in Soil and 'Validation Assessment of In Vitro Arsenic Bioaccessibility Assay for Predicting Relative Bioavailability of Arsenic in Soils and Soil-like Materials at Superfund Sites.'" OLEM 9355.4-29, April 20. Washington, DC: EPA. https://clu-in.org/download/contaminantfocus/arsenic/arsenic-OLEM-9355.4-29.pdf.

DUST SAMPLE COLLECTION

ASTM International. 2018. "ASTM D6966-18, Standard Practice for Collection of Settled Dust Samples Using Wipe Sampling Methods for Subsequent Determination of Metals." West Conshohocken, PA: ASTM International. https://www.astm.org/Standards/D6966.htm.

ASTM International. 2020. "ASTM E1728-20, Standard Practice for Collection of Settled Dust Samples Using Wipe Sampling Methods for Subsequent Lead Determination." West Conshohocken, PA: ASTM International. https://www.astm.org/Standards/E1728.htm.

EPA (US Environmental Protection Agency). 1966. "Analysis of Composite Wipe Samples for Lead Content." EPA 747-R-96-003. Washington, DC: EPA.

Friederich, N. J., M. Karin, K. M. Bauer, B. D. Schultz, and T. S. Holderman. 1999. "The Use of Composite Dust Wipe Samples as a Means of Assessing Lead Exposure." *American Industrial Hygiene Association Journal* 60 (3): 326–33. doi:10.1080/00028899908984449.

HUD (US Department of Housing and Urban Development). 2012. "Wipe Sampling of Settled Dust for Lead Determination." In *Guidelines for the Evaluation and Control of Lead-Based Paint Hazards in Housing*, 2nd ed., Appendix 13.1. Washington, DC: HUD. https://www.hud.gov/sites/documents/LBPH-40.PDF

APPENDIX D

Biomonitoring Resources

Biomonitoring and biological-sample collection should be conducted under the supervision of a trained professional, and most institutional review boards and ethics-review organizations will make that a prerequisite to data collection. This appendix provides links to accepted methods for sample collection across biological matrices, as well as information on efforts worldwide to coordinate biomonitoring programs.

Table D.1 provides an overview of biomonitoring studies conducted in low- and middle-income countries (LMICs).

TABLE D.1 Selected biomonitoring studies for lead, metals, and mercury with application to LMICs

REFERENCE	LOCATION	INDUSTRY	POLLUTANT	BIOLOGICAL MATRIX	ANALYTICAL METHOD	ANALYTICAL LAB	NOTES
Lead							
Baghurst et al. (1992)	Port Pirie, South Australia	Lead smelter	Lead	Capillary blood	Electrothermal atomization atomic absorption spectrometry	Department of Chemical Pathology at Adelaide Centre for Women's and Children's Health	Cited prior study showing close correlation ($r = 0.97$) b/w capillary and venous sampling (Calder et al. 1986)
Malcoe et al. (2002)	Northeastern Oklahoma	Lead and zinc mining	Lead	Venous blood	Graphite furnace atomic absorption spectrometry	Samples shipped to Oklahoma State Department of Health laboratory	
Jones et al. (2011)	Senegal (Thiaroye Sur Mer)	Lead-acid battery disposal	Lead	(1) Venous blood (2) Capillary blood	(1) Graphite furnace atomic absorption spectrometry (2) LeadCare portable test kits	(1) Samples shipped to Pasteur Cerba-certified lab (France) (2) In field	"HI" LeadCare readings sent to lab

continued

TABLE D.1, *continued*

REFERENCE	LOCATION	INDUSTRY	POLLUTANT	BIOLOGICAL MATRIX	ANALYTICAL METHOD	ANALYTICAL LAB	NOTES
Lo et al. (2012)	Zamfara State, Nigeria	Gold-ore processing	Lead	Venous blood	LeadCare II portable analyzer	Samples were analyzed at the Blood Lead and Inorganic Metals Lab (Gusau, Zamfara)	Product lots of all blood collection supplies were prescreened for lead contamination by CDC labs, and supplies were stored in plastic bags before collection to prevent in-field contamina-tion
Caravanos et al. (2014)	Kabwe, Zambia	Lead mining and smelting	Lead	Capillary blood	LeadCare II portable analyzer	In field	
Gao et al. (2001)	Wuxi City, China	n.a.	Lead	Capillary blood	Graphite furnace atomic absorption spectrometry	Shipped to School of Public Health, Beijing Medical University	
Riddell et al. (2007); Solon et al. (2008)	Central Philippines	n.a.	Lead	Venous blood	LeadCare analyzer; subset analyzed using atomic absorption spectroscopy	Samples were analyzed at a central laboratory in Manila	Cited previous field work demonstrating good correlation ($r = 0.829$) between LeadCare device and atomic absorption spectrometry (Counter et al. 1998); study also measured hemoglobin (HemoCue Blood Hemoglobin Photometer) and red blood cell folate (Architect system)
Xie et al. (2013)	China (16 cities)	n.a.	Lead	Capillary blood	BH2100 tungsten atomizer absorp-tion spectropho-tometer	n.a.	QA/QC program for blood lead levels higher than 10 ug/dL (used double test method)
Daniell et al. (2015)	Hung Yen Province, northern Vietnam	Battery recycling	Lead	Capillary blood	LeadCare II portable analyzer	In field	Children only; confirmatory venous sampling for high field levels; extensive soil, survey, medical data also collected
Grigoryan et al. (2016)	Northern Armenia	Metal mining and smelting	Lead	Capillary blood	LeadCare II portable analyzer	In field	Blood samples collected following CDC recommended finger-stick method; cites results of CLIA waiver clinical field trials that found good correlation ($r = 0.979$) between this device and graphite furnace atomic absorption spectrometry (GFAAS)

continued

TABLE D.1, *continued*

REFERENCE	LOCATION	INDUSTRY	POLLUTANT	BIOLOGICAL MATRIX	ANALYTICAL METHOD	ANALYTICAL LAB	NOTES
Metals							
Were et al. (2008)	Nairobi, Kenya	School-age children in industrial areas	Lead, cadmium, calcium, zinc, and iron	Fingernails	Atomic absorption spectrometer with acid digestion	Kenyatta University Research Laboratory and Mines and Geology Analytical Research Department, Nairobi	
Qu et al. (2012)	Jiangsu Province, China	Lead-zinc mining	Metals	Hair	Inductively coupled argon plasma mass spectrometry (USEPA 6020A) for metals Thermal decomposition, amalgamation, and atomic absorption spectrophotometry (USEPA 7473) for Hg	—	Ag, Cd, Cr, Cu, Ni, Pb, Se, Ti, Zn, Hg; notes that hair useful for assessing long-term exposure and for certain metals (Pb, Hg) but not others (Zn, Cu, Cd)
Thakur et al. (2010)	Punjab, India	Wastewater drains	Metals, pesticides	Blood Urine Human milk	Community-based interviews of women and children; clinical examination and records review by medical doctors of selected cases	—	Urine (Hg, Cd, Pb, As, Se) Blood/milk (pesticides)
Röllin et al. (2009)	South Africa	Multiple (for example, industrial and mining sites)	Metals	Venous blood (before delivery) Umbilical cord blood	Element 2 mass spectrometer	Samples shipped to University of Tromso, Norway, and analyzed at National Institute for Occupational Health	Cd, Hg, Pb, Mn, CO, Cu, Zn, As, Se
Banza et al. (2009)	Congo, Dem. Rep.	Metal mining and smelting	Metals	Urine (spot)	Inductively coupled argon plasma mass spectrometry	Samples analyzed in Laboratory of Industrial Toxicology and Occupational Medicine Unit (Belgium)	Al, Sb, As, Cd, Cr, Co, Cu, Pb, Mn, Mo, Ni, Se, Te, Sn, U, V, Zn; creatinine adjusted
Ibeto and Okoye (2010)	Enugu State, Nigeria	n.a.	Metals	Venous blood	GBC atomic absorption spectrophotometer	University of Nigeria Nsukka, Enugu State	Ni, Mn, Cr
Alatise and Schrauzer (2010)	Nigeria, Africa	n.a.	Metals	Blood (fasting) Hair (scalp) Breast biopsy	Inductively coupled plasma mass spectrometry	—	Cu, Zn, Pb, Se, Cd, Hg, As, Mn, Sr, Ca, Mg, Li, Co, Zn/Cu, Ca/Mg; notes various interactions (for example, Pb interacts with Se and iodine in vivo)

continued

TABLE D.1, *continued*

REFERENCE	LOCATION	INDUSTRY	POLLUTANT	BIOLOGICAL MATRIX	ANALYTICAL METHOD	ANALYTICAL LAB	NOTES
Caravanos et al. (2013)	Ghana, West Africa	E-waste dumping and recycling	Metals	Urine (first void) Venous blood (serum)	Graphite furnace atomic absorption spectrometry; whole blood spun to isolate cells to produce serum	Ghana Standards Board Forensic Lab in Accra	Ba, Cd, Co, Mn, Cr, Cu, Fe, Hg, Pb, Se, Zn; Sample collection equipment and containers were prescreened or soaked in trace metal-grade nitric acid; analytical flaw in using blood serum because lead resides in erythrocyte
Obiri et al. (2016)	Tarkwa Nsuaem Municipality and the Prestea Huni Valley District, Ghana	Mining	Metals	Whole blood Venous blood (serum)	Neutron activation analysis	Ghana Atomic Energy Commission	As, Cd, Hg, Cu, Pb, Zn, Mn; also administered a health questionnaire. Fasting sample
Sanders et al. (2014)	Red River Delta, Vietnam	Smelting (automobile batteries)	Metals	Capillary blood Toenail	LeadCare II portable analyzer Toenails extracted using modified Method 3050B	In-field toenail samples shipped to RTI International (Research Triangle Park, NC)	In whole blood and serum
Jasso-Pineda et al. (2007)	Villa de la Paz, Mexico	Mining	Metals	Venous blood Urine (first void)	Atomic absorption spectrometry	Universidad Autónoma de San Luis Potosí, Mexico	Blood (lead) Urine (spot)
Nyanza et al. (2019)	Northern Tanzania	ASGM	Arsenic, mercury	Blood (Hg), Urine (As)	Inductively coupled plasma mass spectrometry	ALS Scandinavia Laboratory AB, Luleå. Sweden	Statistically significant differences between artisanal small-scale gold mining (ASGM) and non-ASGM areas
Uriah et al. (2013)	Zamfara State, Nigeria	ASGM	Lead, mercury				
Mercury							
Rodrigues-Filho and Sobral (2004); Bose-O'Reilly et al. (2008, 2010)	North Sulawesi and Central Kalimantan, Indonesia; and Kadoma, Zimbabwe	ASGM	Mercury	Blood Urine (spot) Hair (scalp)	Cold vapor atomic absorption spectrometry	Institute of Forensic Medicine, Munich, Germany	Measured urine Hg, urine Hg creatinine adjusted, blood Hg, total Hg hair, organic Hg hair, and inorganic Hg hair; inorganic Hg burden higher in urine than blood whereas higher blood reflects more exposure to methyl mercury

continued

TABLE D.1, *continued*

REFERENCE	LOCATION	INDUSTRY	POLLUTANT	BIOLOGICAL MATRIX	ANALYTICAL METHOD	ANALYTICAL LAB	NOTES
Marques et al. (2012, 2015)	Rondonia, Brazil	Open-pit tin-ore mining	Mercury	Hair (scalp)	Cold vapor atomic absorption spectrometry	Institute of Biophysics of the Federal University of Rio de Janeiro	Measured total Hg
Sari et al. (2016)	Cihonje, Central Java, Indonesia	ASGM	Mercury	Hair	Cold vapor atomic absorption spectrometry	—	Wastewater, river water, health questionnaire
Wyatt et al. (2017)	Madre de Dios, Peru	ASGM	Mercury	Hair (scalp)	Atomic absorption spectrometry	—	Diet, fish, location, proximity to ASGM
Steckling et al. (2011)	Mongolia	ASGM	Mercury	Blood Urine Hair	Cold vapor atomic absorption spectrometry (urine, hair); inductively coupled plasma mass spectrometry (blood)	National Institute for Minamata Disease, Japan (urine controls); Institute of Forensic Medicine, Munich, Germany (urine exposed); Health and Safety Laboratory, Buxton, United Kingdom (blood)	
Niane et al. (2015)	Kédougou-Kéniéba Inlier, Senegal	ASGM	Mercury	Hair Fish	Atomic absorption spectrometer with acid digestion (hair, fish); Inductively coupled plasma mass spectrometry (fish)	University of Geneva, Switzerland	
Ouboter et al. (2018)	Suriname, South America	ASGM	Mercury	Blood Urine Hair	Cold vapor atomic absorption spectrometry with acid digestion	NZCS/CMO laboratory	Eaton, A. D., L. S. Clesceri, A. W. Greenberg, and M. A. H. Franson. 1998. *Standard Methods for the Examination of Water and Wastewater, 20th ed.* Washington, DC: American Public Health Association, American Water Works Environment Federation.
Vega et al. (2018)	Yanomami village, Brazilian Amazon	ASGM	Mercury	Hair	Inductively coupled plasma mass spectrometry using ICP-MS 7500 CX	Chemistry Department of the Pontificia Universidade Católica in Rio de Janeiro	

continued

TABLE D.1, *continued*

REFERENCE	LOCATION	INDUSTRY	POLLUTANT	BIOLOGICAL MATRIX	ANALYTICAL METHOD	ANALYTICAL LAB	NOTES
Sherman et al. (2015)	Kejetia, Ghana, and North Sulawesi, Indonesia	ASGM	Mercury	Urine (spot) Hair (scalp)	Digestion; Direct Mercury Analyzer 80 using EPA method 7473 (thermal decomposition and atomic absorption spectrophotometry; AAS)	—	Total Hg, MeHg, and isotope ratios
Langeland, Hardin, and Neitzel (2017)	Madre de Dios River Basin, Peru	ASGM	Mercury	Hair Fish	Milestone Direct Mercury Analyzer using EPA method 7473 (thermal decomposition and atomic absorption spectrophotometry; AAS)	University of Michigan	
Berky et al. (2019)	Madre de Dios River Basin, Peru	ASGM	Mercury	Hair, Blood	Milestone Direct Mercury Analyzer using EPA method 7473 (thermal decomposition and atomic absorption spectrophotometry; AAS)	University of Michigan	
Yard et al. (2012)	Madre de Dios River Basin, Peru	ASGM	Mercury	Urine (spot) Venous blood (serum)	Inductively coupled dynamic reaction cell plasma mass spectrometry; high-performance liquid chromatography	US CDC (Centers for Disease Control and Prevention) National Center for Environmental Health's Division of Laboratory Sciences in Atlanta, Georgia	
Suvd et al. (2015)	Bornuur and Jargalant soums, Tuv Province, Mongolia	ASGM	Mercury	Urine Venous blood (serum)	Cold vapor atomic absorption spectrometry	Mercury Laboratory of NCPH; Mercury Laboratory of State Professional Inspection Agency, Mongolia	
Pateda, Sakakibara, and Sera (2018)	Gorontalo Province, Indonesia	ASGM	Mercury	Hair (scalp)	Particle-induced X-ray emission (PIXE)	Cyclotron Research Center, Iwate Medical University, Japan	
González-Merizalde et al. (2016)	Nangaritza River Basin, Ecuadorian Amazon	ASGM	Mercury, manganese	Hair (nose and scalp) Urine	Flame atomic absorption spectrometry (Shimadzu 6800), cold vapor atomic absorption spectrometry	—	
Sanchez Rodriguez et al. (2014)	Andes, Colombia	ASGM	Mercury	Blood Urine Hair	Atomic absorption spectrometry (RA-915+)	—	

Source: World Bank compilation.

Note: Bibliographic information for references is listed below. n.a. = not applicable; — = not available; ASGM = artisanal small-scale gold mining. Al = aluminum; As = arsenic; Ba = barium; Ca = calcium; Cd = cadmium; Co = cobalt; Cr = chromium; Cu = copper; Fe = iron; Hg = mercury; Li = lithium; MeHg = methylmercury; Mg = magnesium; Mn = manganese; Mo = molybdenum; Ni = nickel; Pb = lead; Sb = antimony; Se = Selenium; Sn = tin; Sr = strontium; Te = tellurium; Ti = titanium; U = uranium; V = vanadium; Zn = zinc.

SAMPLE-COLLECTION GUIDELINES FOR TRACE ELEMENTS IN BLOOD AND URINE

APHL (Association of Public Health Laboratories). n.d. "Biomonitoring" online resource page includes the National Biomonitoring Network (NBN) of federal, regional, state, and local laboratories that conduct biomonitoring for use in public health practice. APHL, Silver Spring, MD. https://www.aphl.org/programs/environmental_health/nbn/Pages/default .aspx

ATSDR (US Agency for Toxic Substances and Disease Registry). 2020. "Analytical Methods." Discussion of measuring lead in biological matrices in chapter 7 of "Toxicological Profile for Lead," ATSDR, Atlanta. https://www.ncbi.nlm.nih.gov/books/NBK158761/

CDC (US Centers for Disease Control and Prevention). 2006. "CDC Specimen-Collection Protocol for a Chemical-Exposure Event." Infographic, CDC, Atlanta. https://www.health .ny.gov/guidance/oph/wadsworth/chemspecimencollection.pdf.

CDC (US Centers for Disease Control and Prevention). 2013. "Guidelines for Measuring Lead in Blood Using Point of Care Instruments." Guidance from the Advisory Committee on Childhood Lead Poisoning Prevention of the CDC, Atlanta. https://www.cdc.gov/nceh /lead/acclpp/20131024_pocguidelines_final.pdf

CLSI (Clinical Laboratory Standards Institute). 2013. *Measurement Procedures for the Determination of Lead Concentrations in Blood and Urine, 2nd Ed.* CLSI document C40-A2. Wayne, PA: CLSI. https://clsi.org/standards/products/clinical-chemistry-and-toxicology /documents/c40/

Cornelis, R., B. Heinzow, R. F. M. Herber, J. M. Christensen, O. M. Poulsen, E. Sabbioni, D. M. Templeton, Y. Thomassen, M. Vahter, and O. Vesterberg. 1995. "Sample Collection Guidelines for Trace Elements in Blood and Urine." *Pure and Applied Chemistry* 67 (8–9): 1575–1608. http://publications.iupac.org/pac-2007/1995/pdf/6708x1575.pdf.

Cornelis, R., B. Heinzow, R. F. M. Herber, J. M. Christensen, O. M. Poulsen, E. Sabbioni, D. M. Templeton, Y. Thomassen, M. Vahter, and O. Vesterberg. 1996. "Sample Collection Guidelines for Trace Elements in Blood and Urine." *Journal of Trace Elements in Medicine and Biology* 10 (2): 103–27.

EPA (US Environmental Protection Agency). 2019. "Guidelines for Human Exposure Assessment." EPA/100/B-19/001, Risk Assessment Forum. Washington, DC: EPA. https:// www.epa.gov/sites/default/files/2020-01/documents/guidelines_for_human_exposure _assessment_final2019.pdf.

FDA and NIH (US Food and Drug Administration and National Institutes of Health). 2016. "BEST (Biomarkers, EndpointS, and other Tools) Resource." Glossary copublished by the FDA, Silver Spring, MD; and NIH, Bethesda, MD. https://www.ncbi.nlm.nih.gov/books /NBK326791/pdf/Bookshelf_NBK326791.pdf

Heppner, Claudia. 2011. "Biomarkers in Risk Assessment: Application for Chemical Contaminants." PowerPoint presentation at the EU Decision Makers Meeting, "Use of Human Biomonitoring for Policy Making," Munich, May 4. http://www.eu-hbm.info /cophes/4_Biomarkersinriskassessment.pdf

IPCS (International Programme on Chemical Safety). 1993. *Biomarkers and Risk Assessment: Concepts and Principles.* Environmental Health Criteria (EHC) 155. Geneva: World Health Organization. http://apps.who.int/iris/bitstream/handle/10665/39037/9241571551-eng .pdf;jsessionid=77D78AFFF865ABE58A666BB4941A9330?sequence=1

MEASURE Evaluation. 2000. "Biological and Clinical Data Collection in Population Surveys in Less Developed Countries." Summary of MEASURE Evaluation meeting, National Academy of Sciences, Washington, DC, January 24–25. https://www.who.int/hiv/pub/surveillance /en/biomarkers.pdf?ua=1.

WHO (World Health Organization). 2010. *WHO Guidelines on Drawing Blood: Best Practices in Phlebotomy.* Geneva: WHO. https://www.euro.who.int/__data/assets/pdf_file /0005/268790/WHO-guidelines-on-drawing-blood-best-practices-in-phlebotomy -Eng.pdf.

WHO (World Health Organization). 2011. *Brief Guide to Analytical Methods for Measuring Lead in Blood.* Geneva: WHO. http://www.who.int/ipcs/assessment/public_health/lead _blood.pdf

Dried blood spots

Crimmins, E., J. K. Kim, H. McCreath, J. Faul, D. Weir, and T. Seeman. 2014. "Validation of Blood-Based Assays Using Dried Blood Spots for Use in Large Population Studies." *Biodemography and Social Biology* 60 (1): 38–48. doi:10.1080/19485565.2014.901885.

Crimmins, E. M., J. D. Faul, J. K. Kim, and D. R. Weir. 2017. "Documentation of Blood-Based Biomarkers in the 2014 Health and Retirement Study." Report, Survey Research Center, Institute for Social Research, University of Michigan, Ann Arbor.

Delahaye, L., B. Janssens, and C. Stove. 2017. "Alternative Sampling Strategies for the Assessment of Biomarkers of Exposure." *Current Opinion in Toxicology* 4: 43–51.

Freeman, J. D., L. M. Rosman, J. D. Ratcliff, P. T. Strickland, D. R. Graham, and E. K. Silbergeld. 2017. "State of the Science in Dried Blood Spots." *Clinical Chemistry* 64 (4): 656–79.

Funk, W. E., J. D. Pleil, D. J. Sauter, T. McDade, and J. L. Holl. 2015. "Use of Dried Blood Spots for Estimating Children's Exposures to Heavy Metals in Epidemiological Research." *Journal of Environmental & Analytical Toxicology* 7 (2): 1–9.

Wagner, M., D. Tonoli, E. Varesio, and G. Hopfgartner. 2016. "The Use of Mass Spectrometry to Analyze Dried Blood Spots." *Mass Spectrometry Reviews* 35 (3): 361–438.

Cardiovascular (C-reactive protein)

Ahn, J. S., S. Choi, S. H. Jang, H. J. Chang, J. H. Kim, K. B. Nahm, S. W. Oh, and E. Y. Choi. 2003. "Development of a Point-of-Care Assay System for High-Sensitivity C-Reactive Protein in Whole Blood." *Clinica Chimica Acta* 332 (1–2): 51–59.

Brindle, E., M. Fujita, J. Shofer, and K. A. O'Connor. 2010. "Serum, Plasma, and Dried Blood Spot High-Sensitivity C-Reactive Protein Enzyme Immunoassay for Population Research." *Journal of Immunological Methods* 362 (1–2): 112–20.

McDade, T. W., J. Burhop, and J. Dohnal. 2004. "High-Sensitivity Enzyme Immunoassay for C-Reactive Protein in Dried Blood Spots." *Clinical Chemistry* 50 (3): 652–54.

Ochoa-Martínez, Á. C., E. D. Cardona-Lozano, L. Carrizales-Yáñez, and I. N. Pérez-Maldonado. 2018. "Serum Concentrations of New Predictive Cardiovascular Disease Biomarkers in Mexican Women Exposed to Lead." *Archives of Environmental Contamination and Toxicology* 74 (2): 248–58.

Peña, M. S. B., and A. Rollins. 2017. "Environmental Exposures and Cardiovascular Disease: A Challenge for Health and Development in Low- and Middle-Income Countries." *Cardiology Clinics* 35 (1): 71–86.

Roberts, W. L., L. Moulton, T. C. Law, G. Farrow, M. Cooper-Anderson, J. Savory, and N. Rifai. 2001. "Evaluation of Nine Automated High-Sensitivity C-Reactive Protein Methods: Implications for Clinical and Epidemiological Applications. Part 2." *Clinical Chemistry* 47 (3): 418–25.

Roberts, W. L., E. L. Schwarz, S. Ayanian, and N. Rifai. 2001, "Performance Characteristics of a Point of Care C-Reactive Protein Assay." *Clinica Chimica Acta* 314 (1–2): 255–59.

Roberts W. L., R. Sedrick, L. Moulton, A. Spencer, and N. Rifai. 2000. "Evaluation of Four Automated High-Sensitivity C-Reactive Protein Methods: Implications for Clinical and Epidemiological Applications." *Clinical Chemistry* 46 (4): 461–68.

Point-of-care (POC) and In-field diagnostic assays and methods

Byrnes, S., G. Thiessen, and E. Fu. 2013. "Progress in the Development of Paper-Based Diagnostics for Low-Resource Point-of-Care Settings." *Bioanalysis* 5 (22): 2821–36.

Drain, P. K., E. P. Hyle, F. Noubary, K. A. Freedberg, D. Wilson, W. R. Bishai, W. Rodriguez, and I. V. Bassett. 2014. "Diagnostic Point-of-Care Tests in Resource-Limited Settings." *Lancet Infectious Diseases* 14 (3): 239–49.

Garcia, P. J., P. You, G. Fridley, D. Mabey, and R. Peeling. 2015. "Point-of-Care Diagnostic Tests for Low-Resource Settings." *Lancet Global Health* 3 (5): e257–8.

Gubala, V., L. F. Harris, A. J. Ricco, M. X .Tan, and D. E. Williams. 2011. "Point of Care Diagnostics: Status and Future." *Analytical Chemistry* 84 (2): 487–515.

Sharma, S., J. Zapatero-Rodríguez, P. Estrela, and R. O'Kennedy. 2015. "Point-of-Care Diagnostics in Low Resource Settings: Present Status and Future Role of Microfluidics." *Biosensors* 5 (3): 577–601.

Shaw, J. L. 2016. "Practical Challenges Related to Point of Care Testing." *Practical Laboratory Medicine* 4: 22–29.

Song, Y., Y. Y. Huang, X. Liu, X. Zhang, M. Ferrari, and L. Qin. 2014. "Point-of-Care Technologies for Molecular Diagnostics Using a Drop of Blood." *Trends in Biotechnology* 32 (3): 132–39.

St. John, A., and C. P. Price. 2014. "Existing and Emerging Technologies for Point-of-Care Testing." *Clinical Biochemist Reviews* 35 (3): 155–67.

Vashist, S. K., P. B. Luppa, L. Y. Yeo, A. Ozcan, and J. H. Luong. 2015. "Emerging Technologies for Next-Generation Point-of-Care Testing." *Trends in Biotechnology* 33 (11): 692–705.

Xu, X., A. Akay, H. Wei, S. Wang, B. Pingguan-Murphy, B. E. Erlandsson, X. Li et al. 2015. "Advances in Smartphone-Based Point-of-Care Diagnostics." *Proceedings of the IEEE* 103 (2): 236–47.

MODELING TOOLS

A variety of modeling approaches are available for quantifying and predicting contaminant fate, transport, and external and internal exposures from source to outcome, as presented in the conceptual site model (CSM). Fate and transport models are used to quantify the movement of contaminants through environmental media to the point of exposure. For example, air-quality models predict wet and dry deposition of airborne contaminants from a variety of sources based on local estimates of wind speed, rainfall, and other parameters. Similarly, groundwater models predict expected concentrations in groundwater from leaching in soils or other mechanisms. These models could be used together with measured soil concentrations (chapter 3) and site-specific parameters to predict groundwater concentrations, which could then be verified using groundwater measurements (chapter 3).

There are many different models that could be applied along the continuum from contaminant source to health outcome, and they vary in complexity and required inputs. This appendix provides links to resources to consult in deciding which models to use and identifies a limited set of specific models relevant to assessing exposure to metals in low- and middle-income countries (LMICs). For example, the integrated exposure uptake biokinetic model for lead in children (IEUBK) is a model developed by the US Environmental Protection Agency (EPA) to predict expected blood lead levels in children from measured concentrations in soil. This model, together with LMIC-specific exposure factors (appendix B), could be combined to predict the biomonitoring data (chapter 4). Similarly, several physiologically based pharmacokinetic (PBPK) models exist to link external exposure concentrations (chapter 3) to internal concentrations in target organs, tissues, and blood, which can then be verified in a limited way (for example, blood, urine, hair) using biomonitoring data (chapter 4). This may allow for less data collection in the future or achieve other goals.

Depending on the model's complexity, some degree of training and experience with specific models is generally required to gain proficiency with their use. Models generally require site-specific calibration and verification to effectively support decision-making.

EPA (US Environmental Protection Agency). 2021. "Integrated Exposure Uptake Biokinetic Model for Lead in Children, Windows® version (IEUBKwin v2) (May 2021) 32/64-bit version." Software, EPA, Washington, DC.

The Integrated Exposure Uptake Biokinetic (IEUBK) Model for Lead in Children is stand-alone, Windows-based software developed by the US EPA. The model predicts the distribution of expected blood lead concentrations for a hypothetical child or population of children based on measured or assumed concentrations of Pb in the environment, particularly soil and drinking water (chapter 3). From this distribution, the model calculates the probability that predicted blood lead concentrations will exceed a user-defined level of concern (default 10 μg/dL). The user can then explore an array of possible changes in exposure media that would reduce the probability that blood lead concentrations would be above this level of concern. Beginning in 1990, the model has undergone many iterations and review cycles, and has been well vetted in the literature and elsewhere.

The model is optimized for children less than seven years old who are exposed to environmental Pb from many sources. The model can also be used to predict cleanup levels for various media assuming residential land use. Studies show that the model is most sensitive to the amount of soil and dust ingested per day. In decreasing order of sensitivity, predicted Pb uptake is moderately sensitive to the assumed absorption fraction for soil/dust and diet, the soil Pb concentration, the indoor dust Pb concentration, dietary-lead concentration, contribution of soil lead to indoor dust lead, and the half-saturation absorbable intake (based on output-input ratio). Finally, the predicted probability of exceeding a specified level of concern is highly sensitive to changes in the geometric standard deviation (GSD). The GSD is a measure of the variability among individuals who have contact with a fixed lead concentration and is based on analyses of data from neighborhoods having paired sets of environmental concentration and blood Pb data from high-income countries (HICs). This value likely differs for LMICs.

EPA (US Environmental Protection Agency). n.d. "Lead at Superfund Sites: Frequent Questions from Risk Assessors. on the Adult Lead Model Methodology. Questions, Input Variables, and Application" EPA, Washington, DC.

While the IEUBK model is designed for children, the Adult Lead Model (ALM) focuses on adults. The required inputs are similar, but the ALM model is designed for adult populations.

Physiologically based pharmacokinetic (PBPK) models for metals

PBPK models are contaminant-specific and typically are used to evaluate contaminant disposition in the human body following exposure. The models are generally based on studies in which animals, often rodents, are exposed to known quantities of contaminants via specific exposure routes and the animals are sacrificed at various time points and organ-specific contaminant concentrations are assessed. The animal data relate to humans through a comparison of physiological-rate constants (for example, breathing rate, blood volume, and so on).

Kenyon, E. M., and H. J. Clewell III. 2015. "Toxicokinetics and Pharmacokinetic Modeling of Arsenic." In *Arsenic: Exposure Sources, Health Risks, and Mechanisms of Toxicity*, edited by J. C. States, 495–510. Hoboken, NJ: John Wiley & Sons. https://onlinelibrary.wiley.com/doi/book/10.1002/9781118876992

This book illustrates the chemistry, toxicology, and health effects of As using novel modeling techniques, case studies, experimental data, and future perspectives. Chapter 22 in particular focuses on PBPK modeling for As.

Liao, C. M., T. L. Lin, and S. C. Chen. 2008. "A Weibull-PBPK Model for Assessing Risk of Arsenic-Induced Skin Lesions in Children." *Science of the Total Environment* 392 (2–3): 203–17.

Mumtaz, M., J. Fisher, B. Blount, and P. Ruiz. 2012. "Application of Physiologically Based Pharmacokinetic Models in Chemical Risk Assessment." *Journal of Toxicology.* https://www.ncbi.nlm.nih.gov/pmc/articles/PMC3317240/

Ruiz, P., B. A. Fowler, J. D. Osterloh, J. Fisher, and M. Mumtaz. 2010. "Physiologically Based Pharmacokinetic (PBPK) Tool Kit for Environmental Pollutants–Metals." *SAR and QSAR in Environmental Research* 21 (7–8): 603–18.

Ruiz, P., M. Ray, J. Fisher, and M. Mumtaz. 2011. "Development of a Human Physiologically Based Pharmacokinetic (PBPK) Toolkit for Environmental Pollutants." *International Journal of Molecular Sciences* 12 (11): 7469–80.

Bioaccumulation models

A category of models that may be relevant at artisanal small-scale gold-mining (ASGM) sites is bioaccumulation models (table C.4). These models predict the expected uptake of organic contaminants, specifically methylmercury (MeHg) and other organic contaminants that preferentially partition into the organic fraction of the media they reside in (for example, organic carbon in sediment, lipid in organisms—including humans).

Alatise, Olusegun I., and Gerhard N. Schrauzer. 2010. "Lead Exposure: A Contributing Cause of the Current Breast Cancer Epidemic in Nigerian Women." *Biological Trace Element Research* 136: 127–39.

Baghurst, Peter A., Anthony J. McMichael, Neil R. Wigg, Graham V. Vimpani, Evelyn F. Robertson, Russell J. Roberts, and Shi-Lu Tong. 1992. "Environmental Exposure to Lead and Children's Intelligence at the Age of Seven Years—The Port Pirie Cohort Study." NEJM 327: 1279–84.

Berky, Alex J., Ian T. Ryde, Beth Feingold, Ernesto J. Ortiz, Lauren H. Wyatt, Caren Weinhouse, Heileen Hsu-Kim, Joel N. Meyer, and William K. Pan. 2019. "Predictors of Mitochondrial DNA Copy Number and Damage in a Mercury-Exposed Rural Peruvian Population near Artisanal and Small-Scale Gold Mining: An Exploratory Study." *Environ. Mol. Mutagen* 60: 197–210.

Bose-O'Reilly, Stephan, Gustav Drasch, Christian Beinhoff, Saulo Rodrigues-Filho, Gabriel Roider, Beate Lettmeier, Alexandra Maydl, Stefan Maydl, and Uwe Siebert. 2010. "Health Assessment of Artisanal Gold Miners in Indonesia." *Science of The Total Environment* 408 (4): 713–25.

Bose-O'Reilly, Stephan, Beate Lettmeier, Raffaella Matteucci Gothe, Christian Beinhoff, Uwe Siebert, and Gustav Drasch. 2008. "Mercury as a Serious Health Hazard for Children in Gold Mining Areas." *Environmental Research* 107 (1): 89–97.

Calder, Ian C., David M. Roder, Adrian J. Esterman, Milton J. Lewis, Malcolm C. Harrison, and Robert K. Oldfield. 1986. "Blood Lead Levels in Children in the North-West of Adelaide." *Medical Journal of Australia* 144 (10): 509–12.

Caravanos, Jack, Edith E. Clarke, Carl S. Osei, and Yaw Amoyaw-Osei. 2013. "Exploratory Health Assessment of Chemical Exposures at E-Waste Recycling and Scrapyard Facility in Ghana." *Journal of Health and Pollution* 3 (4): 11–22. https://doi.org/10.5696/2156-9614-3.4.11.

Caravanos, Jack, Russell Dowling, Martha María Téllez-Rojo Dra, Alejandra Cantoral, Roni Kobrosly, Daniel Estrada, Manuela Orjuela, Sandra Gualtero, Bret Ericson, Anthony Rivera, and Richard Fuller. 2014. "Blood Lead Levels in Mexico and Pediatric Burden of Disease Implications." *Annals of Global Health* 80 (4): 269–77.

Counter, S. A., L. H. Buchanan, G. Laurell, and F. Ortega. 1998. "Field Screening of Blood Lead Levels in Remote Andean Villages." *Neurotoxicology* 19 (6): 871–77.

Daniell, William E., Lo Van Tung, Ryan M. Wallace, Deborah J. Havens, Catherine J. Karr, Nguyen Bich Diep, Gerry A. Croteau, Nancy J. Beaudet, and Nguyen Duy Bao. 2015. "Childhood Lead Exposure from Battery Recycling in Vietnam." *BioMed Research International* 2015: 193715. http://dx.doi.org/10.1155/2015/193715.

Gao, Wanzhen, Zhu Lia, Rachel B. Kaufmann, Robert L. Jones, Zhengang Wang, Yafen Chen, Xiuqin Zhao, and Naifen Wang. 2001. "Blood Lead Levels among Children Aged 1 to 5 Years in Wuxi City, China." *Environmental Research* 87 (1): 11–19.

González-Merizalde, Max V., José A. Menezes-Filho, Claudia Teresa Cruz-Erazo, Santos Amable Bermeo-Flores, María Obdulia Sánchez-Castillo, David Hernández-Bonilla, and Abrahan Mora. 2016. "Manganese and Mercury Levels in Water, Sediments, and Children Living Near Gold-Mining Areas of the Nangaritza River Basin, Ecuadorian Amazon." *Archives of Environmental Contamination and Toxicology* 71: 171–82.

Grigoryan, Ruzanna, Varduhi Petrosyan, Dzovinar Melkom Melkomian, Vahe Khachadourian, Andrew McCartor, and Byron Crape. 2016. "Risk Factors for Children's Blood Lead Levels in Metal Mining and Smelting Communities in Armenia: A Cross-Sectional Study." *BMC Public Health* 16: 945. doi:10.1186/s12889-016-3613-9.

Ibeto, C. N., and C. O. B. Okoye. 2010. "High Levels of Heavy Metals in Blood of the Urban Population in Nigeria." *Research Journal of Environmental Sciences* 4 (4): 371– 82.

Jasso-Pineda, Yolanda, Guillermo Espinosa-Reyes, Donají González-Mille, Israel Razo-Soto, Leticia Carrizales, Arturo Torres-Dosal, Jesús Mejía-Saavedra, Marcos Monroy, Ana Irina Ize, Mario Yarto, and Fernando Díaz-Barriga. 2007. "An Integrated Health Risk Assessment Approach to the Study of Mining Sites Contaminated with Arsenic and Lead." *Integrated Environmental Assessment and Management* 3 (3): 344–50.

Jones, Donald E., Assane Diop, Meredith Block, Alexander Smith-Jones, and Andrea Smith-Jones. 2011. "Assessment and Remediation of Lead Contamination in Senegal." *Blacksmith Institute Journal of Health & Pollution* 1 (2): 37–47.

Langeland, A. L., R. D. Hardin, and R. L. Neitzel. 2017. "Mercury Levels in Human Hair and Farmed Fish Near Artisanal and Small-Scale Gold Mining Communities in the Madre de Dios River Basin, Peru." *Int. J. Environ. Res. Public Health* 14 (3): 302. https://doi.org/10.3390/ijerph14030302.

Lo, Yi-Chun, Carrie A. Dooyema, Antonio Neri, James Durant, Taran Jefferies, Andrew Medina-Marino, Lori de Ravello, Douglas Thoroughman, Lora Davis, Raymond S. Dankoli, Matthias Y. Samson, Luka M. Ibrahim, Ossai Okechukwu, Nasir T. Umar-Tsafe, Alhassan H. Dama, and Mary Jean Brown. 2012. "Childhood Lead Poisoning Associated with Gold Ore Processing: A Village-Level Investigation—Zamfara State, Nigeria, October–November 2010." *Environmental Health Perspectives* 120 (10): 1450–55.

Malcoe, Lorraine Halinka, Robert A. Lynch, Michelle Crozier Keger, and Valerie J Skaggs. 2002. "Lead Sources, Behaviors, and Socioeconomic Factors in Relation to Blood Lead of Native American and White Children: A Community-Based Assessment of a Former Mining Area." *Environmental Health Perspectives* 110 (Supplement 2): 221–31.

Marques, Rejane C., José V. E. Bernardi, Luciana Abreu, José G. Dórea. 2015. "Neurodevelopment Outcomes in Children Exposed to Organic Mercury from Multiple Sources in a Tin-Ore Mine Environment in Brazil." *Archives of Environmental Contamination and Toxicology* 68: 432–41.

Marques, Rejane C., José G. Dórea, Renata S. Leão, Verusca G. dos Santos, Lucélia Bueno, Rayson C. Marques, Katiane G. Brandão, Elisabete F. A. Palermo, and Jean Remy D. Guimarães. 2012. "Role of Methylmercury Exposure (from Fish Consumption) on Growth and Neurodevelopment of Children Under 5 Years of Age Living in a Transitioning (Tin-Mining) Area of the Western Amazon, Brazil." *Archives of Environmental Contamination and Toxicology* 62: 341–50.

Niane, Birane, Stéphane Guédron, Robert Moritz, Claudia Cosio, Papa Malick Ngom, Naresh Deverajan, Hans Rudolf Pfeifer, and John Poté. 2015. "Human Exposure to Mercury in Artisanal Small-Scale Gold Mining Areas of Kedougou Region, Senegal, as a Function of Occupational Activity and Fish Consumption." *Environmental Science and Pollution Research* 22: 7101–11.

Nyanza, Elias C., François P. Bernier, Mange Manyama, Jennifer Hatfield, Jonathan W. Martin, and Deborah Dewey. 2019. "Maternal Exposure to Arsenic and Mercury in Small-Scale Gold Mining Areas of Northern Tanzania." *Environmental Research* 173 (June): 432–42.

Obiri, Samuel, Precious A. D. Mattah, Memuna M. Mattah, Frederick A. Armah, Shiloh Osae, Sam Adu-kumi, and Philip O. Yeboah. 2016. "Assessing the Environmental and Socio-Economic Impacts of Artisanal Gold Mining on the Livelihoods of Communities in the Tarkwa Nsuaem Municipality in Ghana." *Int. J. Environ. Res. Public Health* 13 (2): 160. https://doi.org/10.3390/ijerph13020160.

Ouboter, Paul E., Gwendolyn Landburg, Gaitrie U. Satnarain, Sheryl Y. Starke, Indra Nanden, Bridget Simon-Friedt, William B. Hawkins, Robert Taylor, Maureen Y. Lichtveld, Emily Harville, and Jeffrey K. Wickliffe. 2018. "Mercury Levels in Women and Children from Interior Villages in Suriname, South America." *Int. J. Environ. Res. Public Health* 15: 1007. doi:10.3390/ijerph15051007.

Pateda, S. M., M. Sakakibara, and K. Sera. 2018. "Lung Function Assessment as an Early Biomonitor of Mercury-Induced Health Disorders in Artisanal and Small-Scale Gold Mining Areas in Indonesia." *Int. J. Environ. Res. Public Health* 15 (11): 2480. https://doi.org/10.3390/ijerph15112480.

Qu, Chang-Sheng, Zong-Wei Ma, Jin Yang, Yang Liu, Jun Bi, and Lei Huang. 2012. "Human Exposure Pathways of Heavy Metals in a Lead-Zinc Mining Area, Jiangsu Province, China." *PLOS ONE* 7 (11) e46793.

Riddell, Travis J, Orville Solon, Stella A. Quimbo, Cheryl May C. Tan, Elizabeth Butrick, and John W. Peabody. 2007. "Elevated Blood-Lead Levels among Children Living in the Rural Philippines." *Bulletin of the World Health Organization* 85 (9): 674–82.

Rodrigues-Filho, Saulo, and Luis Gonzaga Sobral. 2004. "7th International Conference on Mercury as a Global Pollutant: Panelists' Report." *Journal of Soils and Sediments* 4 (3): 197–200.

Röllin, Halina B., Cibele V. C. Rudge, Yngvar Thomassen, Angela Mathee, and Jon Ø. Odland. 2009. "Levels of Toxic and Essential Metals in Maternal and Umbilical Cord Blood from Selected Areas of South Africa—Results of a Pilot Study." *J. Environ. Monit.* 11: 618–27.

Sánchez Rodríguez, Luz Helena, Oscar Flórez-Vargas, Laura Andrea Rodríguez-Villamizar, Yolanda Vargas Fiallo, Elena E. Stashenko, and Gerardo Ramírez. 2014. "Lack of Autoantibody Induction by Mercury Exposure in Artisanal Gold Mining Settings in Colombia: Findings and a Review of the Epidemiology Literature." *Journal of Immunotoxicology* 12 (4): 368–75. doi:10.3109/1547691X.2014.986591.

Sanders, Alison P., Sloane K. Miller, Viet Nguyen, Jonathan B. Kotch, and Rebecca C. Fry. 2014. "Toxic Metal Levels in Children Residing in a Smelting Craft Village in Vietnam: A Pilot Biomonitoring Study." *BMC Public Health* 14: 114.

Sari, Mega M., Takanobu Inoue, Yoshitaka Matsumoto, and Kuriko Yokota. 2016. "Measuring Total Mercury Due to Small-Scale Gold Mining Activities to Determine Community Vulnerability in Cihonje, Central Java, Indonesia." *Water Sci. Technol.* 73 (2): 437–44. https://doi.org/10.2166/wst.2015.503.

Sherman, Laura S., Joel D. Blum, Niladri Basu, Mozhgon Rajaee, David C. Evers, David G. Buck, Jindrich Petrlik, and Joseph DiGangi. 2015. "Assessment of Mercury Exposure among Small-Scale Gold Miners Using Mercury Stable Isotopes." *Environmental Research* 137 (February): 226–34.

Solon, Orville, Travis J. Riddell, Stella A. Quimbo, Elizabeth Butrick, Glen P. Aylward, Marife Lou Bacate, and John W. Peabody. 2008. "Associations between Cognitive Function, Blood Lead Concentration, and Nutrition among Children in the Central Philippines." *Journal of Pediatrics* 152 (2): 237–43.

Steckling, Nadine, Stephan Boese-O'Reilly, Cornelia Gradel, Kersten Gutschmidt, Enkhtsetseg Shinee, Enkhjargal Altangerel, Burmaa Badrakh, Ichinkhorloo Bonduush, Unursaikhan Surenjav, Philip Ferstl, Gabriele Roider, Mineshi Sakamoto, Ovnair Sepai, Gustav Drasch, Beate Lettmeier, Jackie Morton, Kate Jones, Uwe Siebertak, and Claudia Hornberg. 2011. "Mercury Exposure in Female Artisanal Small-Scale Gold Miners (ASGM) in Mongolia: An Analysis of Human Biomonitoring (HBM) Data from 2008." *Science of The Total Environment* 409 (5): 994–1000.

Suvd, Duvjir Suvd, Rendoo Davaadorj, Dayanjav Baatartsol, Surenjav Unursaikhan, Myagmar Tsengelmaa, Tsogbayar Oyu, Sonom Yunden, Ana M. Hagan-Rogers, and Stephan Böse-O'Reilly. 2015. "Toxicity Assessment in Artisanal Miners from Low-Level Mercury Exposure in Bornuur and Jargalant Soums of Mongolia." *Procedia Environmental Sciences* 30: 97–102.

Thakur, Jarnail Singh, Shankar Prinja, Dalbir Singh, Arvind Rajwanshi, Rajendra Prasad, Harjinder Kaur Parwana, and Rajesh Kumar. 2010. "Adverse Reproductive and Child Health Outcomes among People Living near Highly Toxic Waste Water Drains in Punjab, India." *J. Epidemiol. Community Health* 64: 148e–154. doi:10.1136/jech.2008.078568.

Uriah, Lar, Tsuwang Kenneth, Gusikit Rhoda, and Mangs Ayuba. 2013. "Lead and Mercury Contamination Associated with Artisanal Gold Mining in Anka, Zamfara State, North Western Nigeria: The Continued Unabated Zamfara Lead Poisoning." *Journal of Earth Science and Engineering* 3: 764–75.

Vega, Claudia M., Jesem D. Y. Orellana, Marcos W. Oliveira, Sandra S. Hacon, and Paulo C. Basta. 2018. "Human Mercury Exposure in Yanomami Indigenous Villages from the Brazilian Amazon." *Int. J. Environ. Res. Public Health* 15 (6): 1051. https://doi.org/10.3390/ijerph15061051.

Were, Faridah Hussein, Wilson Njue, Jane Murung, and Ruth Wanjau. 2008. "Use of Human Nails as Bio-Indicators of Heavy Metals Environmental Exposure among School Age Children in Kenya." *Science of The Total Environment* 393 (2–3): 376–84.

Wyatt, Lauren, Ernesto J. Ortiz, Beth Feingold, Axel Berky, Sarah Diringer, Ana Maria Morales, Elvis Rojas Jurado, Heileen Hsu-Kim, and William Pan. 2017. "Spatial, Temporal, and Dietary Variables Associated with Elevated Mercury Exposure in Peruvian Riverine Communities Upstream and Downstream of Artisanal and Small-Scale Gold Mining." *Int. J. Environ. Res. Public Health* 14 (12): 1582. https://doi.org/10.3390/ijerph14121582.

Xie, Xiao-hua, Zang-wen Tan, Ni Jia, Zhao-yang Fan, Shuai-ming Zhang, Yan-yu Lü, Li Chen, and Yao-hua Dai. 2013. "Blood Lead Levels among Children Aged 0 to 6 Years in 16 Cities of China, 2004–2008." Chinese Medical Journal 126 (12): 2291–95. doi:10.3760/cma.j.issn .0366-6999.20122327

Yard, Ellen E., Jane Horton, Joshua G. Schier, Kathleen Caldwell, Carlos Sanchez, Lauren Lewis, and Carmen Gastañaga. 2012. "Mercury Exposure Among Artisanal Gold Miners in Madre de Dios, Peru: A Cross-sectional Study." *J. Med. Toxicol.* 8: 441–48.

APPENDIX E

Resources for Health-Outcomes Assessment

This appendix provides links to resources for evaluating methods for assessing specific health outcomes (see Bickley 2012 below and table E.1). Note that intermediate health outcomes evaluated using biomarkers are discussed in chapter 4 and appendix D, which focus on sampling in biological matrices for biomarkers of exposure, effect, or both exposure and effect.

Bickley, L. S. 2012. *Bates' Guide to Examination and History Taking,* 11th ed. Philadelphia: Lippincott Williams & Wilkins, an imprint of Wolters Kluwer.	Interviewing and obtaining a health history

TABLE E.1 Links to resources for health-outcomes assessment

REFERENCE	HEALTH OUTCOME
Pulmonary function testing	
"Pulmonary Function Testing," American Thoracic Society website, https://www.thoracic.org/	Recommended guidelines for pulmonary-function testing (PFT)
Ranu, H., M. Wilde, and B. Madden. 2011. "Pulmonary Function Tests." *Ulster Medical Journal* 80 (2): 84–90. https://www.ncbi.nlm.nih.gov/pmc/articles/PMC3229853/	Overview of PFTs, including references to European and US reference and guidance manuals
Higashimoto, Y., T. Iwata, M. Okada, H. Satoh, K. Fukuda, and Y. Tohda. 2009. "Serum Biomarkers as Predictors of Lung Function Decline in Chronic Obstructive Pulmonary Disease." *Respiratory Medicine* 103 (8): 1231–38. https://www.resmedjournal.com/article/S0954-6111(09)00037-7/fulltext	Discussion of the utility of C-reactive protein (CRP) for predicting lung function
Renal outcomes in children and adults	
National Kidney Foundation website, https://www.kidney.org/	Official guidance from the National Kidney Foundation (US) on standard renal-panel testing and interpretation in urine samples

continued

TABLE E.1, *continued*

REFERENCE	HEALTH OUTCOME
Swedish Council on Health Technology Assessment (SBU). 2013. "Methods to Estimate and Measure Renal Function (Glomerular Filtration Rate): A Systematic Review." Yellow Report No. 214, SBU, Stockholm. https://www.ncbi.nlm.nih.gov/books/NBK285322/pdf/Bookshelf_NBK285322.pdf	Creatinine-based equations from the Modification of Diet in Renal Disease Study (MDRD), the Chronic Kidney Disease Epidemiology Collaboration (CKD-EPI), and the revised Lund-Malmö equation (LM-rev) are all accurate (P30 ≥ 75%) for estimating kidney function in adults, except in patients with GFR < 30 mL/min/1.73 m^2 or BMI < 20 kg/m^2. Cockcroft-Gault (CG) should not be used.
Argyropoulos, C. P., S. S. Chen, Y. H. Ng, M. E Roumelioti, K. Shaffi, P. P. Singh, and A. H. Tzamaloukas. 2017. "Rediscovering Beta-2 Microglobulin as a Biomarker Across the Spectrum of Kidney Diseases." *Frontiers in Medicine* 4: 73. https://www.frontiersin.org/articles/10.3389/fmed.2017.00073/full	Background and justification for use of beta-2-microglobulin as a sensitive marker of kidney damage. This is the preferred biomarker of cadmium (Cd) effects recommended by the European Food Safety Authority (EFSA).

Complete blood count

REFERENCE	HEALTH OUTCOME
Keng, T. B., B. De La Salle, G. Bourner, A. Merino, J.-Y. Han, Y. Kawai, M. T. Peng, R. McCafferty, and International Council for Standardization in Haematology (ICSH). 2016. "Standardization of Haematology Critical Results Management in Adults: An International Council for Standardization in Haematology, ICSH, Survey and Recommendations." *Int j Lab Hematl* 38 (5): 457–71. https://doi.org/10.1111/ijlh.12526	Recommendation for standardization of hematology-reporting units used for complete blood count (CBC)

Neurodevelopmental outcomes in children

REFERENCE	HEALTH OUTCOME
Fernald, L. C. H., E. Prado, P. Kariger, and A. Raikes. 2017. "A Toolkit for Measuring Early Childhood Development in Low- and Middle-Income Countries." World Bank, Washington, DC. https://openknowledge.worldbank.org/handle/10986/29000	Report comes with an Excel spreadsheet to use to help guide selection of appropriate instrument out of 147 possible instruments.
UNESCO (United Nations Educational, Scientific and Cultural Organization). Measuring Early Learning Quality and Outcomes (MELQO). https://www.brookings.edu/wp-content/uploads/2017/06/melqo-measuring-early-learning-quality-outcomes.pdf	Collaborative effort of the MELQO core team, technical advisory groups, and steering committee, describing modules and where they were piloted
Anderson, K., and R. Sayre. 2016. "Measuring Early Learning Quality and Outcomes in Tanzania." Report, Center for Universal Education at Brookings, Washington, DC. https://www.brookings.edu/wp-content/uploads/2017/06/melqo-measuring-early-learning-quality-outcomes-in-tanzania_2016oct.pdf	Application of the MELQO modules and approach in consultation with Ministry of Education in Tanzania, published by the Brookings Institution
Brookings Institution. 2017. "Measuring Early Learning Quality and Outcomes (MELQO)." https://www.brookings.edu/research/measuring-early-learning-quality-and-outcomes-in-tanzania/	Further background and reports on the MELQO effort
World Bank. 2016. "Measuring Early Learning Quality and Outcomes (MELQO) Modules: Quick Guide to Content and Use." https://www.worldbank.org/en/topic/education/brief/ecd-resources	Resource guide for applying the MELQO modules
Abubakar, A., P. Holding, A. Van Baar, C. R. Newton, and F. J. van de Vijver. 2008. "Monitoring Psychomotor Development in a Resource Limited Setting: An Evaluation of the Kilifi Developmental Inventory." *Annals of Tropical Paediatrics* 28 (3): 217–26. https://ora.ox.ac.uk/objects/uuid:b6a43d8c-0d7e-4e01-a2ba-521e4ae33c55	Overview of a psychomotor-testing instrument for use in limited-resource settings
Ballot, D. E., T. Ramdin, D. Rakotsoane, F. Agaba, V. A. Davies, T. Chirwa, and P. A. Cooper. 2017. "Use of the Bayley Scales of Infant and Toddler Development, Third Edition, to Assess Developmental Outcome in Infants and Young Children in an Urban Setting in South Africa." *International Scholarly Research Notices* 2017 (2): 1631760. https://www.ncbi.nlm.nih.gov/pmc/articles/PMC5556991/	Example of an adaptation of a standardized instrument, the Bayley Scales, to South Africa
Dramé, C., and C. J. Ferguson. 2019. "Measurements of Intelligence in Sub-Saharan Africa: Perspectives Gathered from Research in Mali." *Current Psychology* 38: 110–15. https://link.springer.com/article/10.1007/s12144-017-9591-y	Discussion of neurodevelopmental testing approaches used in Mali
Ertem, I. O., D. G. Dogan, C. G. Gok, S. U. Kizilates, A. Caliskan, G. Atay, N. Vatandas, T. Karaaslan, S. G. Baskan, and D. V. Cicchetti. 2008. "A Guide for Monitoring Child Development in Low- and Middle-Income Countries." *Pediatrics* 121 (3): e581–89. https://pediatrics.aappublications.org/content/121/3/e581.short	Overview of testing instruments that have been adapted to low-resource settings

continued

TABLE E.1, *continued*

REFERENCE	HEALTH OUTCOME
Gladstone, M. J., G. A. Lancaster, A. P. Jones, K. Maleta, E. Mtitimila, P. Ashorn, and R. L. Smyth. 2008. "Can Western Developmental Screening Tools be Modified for Use in a Rural Malawian Setting?" *Archives of Disease in Childhood* 93 (1): 23–29. https://adc.bmj.com/content/archdischild/93/1/23.full.pdf?with-ds=yes	Discussion of potential instruments
Gladstone, M., G. A. Lancaster, E. Umar, M. Nyirenda, E. Kayira, N. R. van den Broek, and R. L. Smyth. 2010. "The Malawi Developmental Assessment Tool (MDAT): The Creation, Validation, and Reliability of a Tool to Assess Child Development in Rural African Settings." *PLoS Medicine* 7 (5): e1000273. https://journals.plos.org/plosmedicine/article?id=10.1371/journal.pmed.1000273	Development and application of a testing instrument in Malawi; could be adapted to other locations
Holding, P. A., H. G. Taylor, S. D. Kazungu, T. Mkala, J. Gona, B. Mwamuye, L. Mbonani, and J. Stevenson. 2004. "Assessing Cognitive Outcomes in a Rural African Population: Development of a Neuropsychological Battery in Kilifi District, Kenya." *Journal of the International Neuropsychological Society* 10 (2): 246–60. https://www.cambridge.org/core/journals/journal-of-the-international-neuropsychological-society/article/abs/assessing-cognitive-outcomes-in-a-rural-african-population-development-of-a-neuropsychological-battery-in-kilifi-district-kenya/7B19180497EA3C84AD41C9C1DF476F77	Experience in Kenya developing an instrument for assessing cognitive development
Janus, M., and D. R. Offord. 2007. "Development and Psychometric Properties of the Early Development Instrument (EDI): A Measure of Children's School Readiness." *Canadian Journal of Behavioural Science* 39 (1): 1–22. https://psycnet.apa.org/buy/2007-04967-001	Although developed in a Western context, the Early Development Instrument (EDI) may be adaptable to low-resource settings
McCoy, D. C, E. D. Peet, M. Ezzati, G. Danaei, M. M. Black, C. R. Sudfeld, W. Fawzi, and G. Fink. 2016. "Early Childhood Developmental Status in Low- and Middle-Income Countries: National, Regional, and Global Prevalence Estimates Using Predictive Modeling." *PLoS Medicine* 4 (1): e1002233. https://journals.plos.org/plosmedicine/article?id=10.1371/journal.pmed.1002034	Early Childhood Development Instrument (ECDI) suitable for young children; well validated in low-resource settings
McCoy, D. C., M. M. Black, B. Daelmans, and T. Dua. 2016. "Measuring Development in Children from Birth to Age 3 at Population Level." *Early Childhood Matters* 125: 34–39. https://bernardvanleer.org/app/uploads/2016/07/Early-Childhood-Matters-2016_6.pdf	Further background on the ECDI instrument
McCoy, D. C., C. R. Sudfeld, D. C. Bellinger, A. Muhihi, G. Ashery, T. E. Weary, W. Fawzi, and G. Fink. 2017. "Development and Validation of an Early Childhood Development Scale for Use in Low-Resourced Settings." *Population Health Metrics* 15 (1): 3. https://pophealthmetrics.biomedcentral.com/articles/10.1186/s12963-017-0122-8	Detailed evaluation of ECDI
Oppong, S. 2017. "Contextualizing Psychological Testing in Ghana." *Psychology and Its Context* 8 (1): 3–17. https://www.researchgate.net/publication/327536906_Contextualizing_psychological_testing_in_Ghana	Discussion of the types of tests used in Ghana and the challenge associated with the current state of psychological testing in Ghana
Sabanathan, S., B. Wills, and M. Gladstone. 2015. "Child Development Assessment Tools in Low-Income and Middle-Income Countries: How Can We Use Them More Appropriately?" *Archives of Disease in Childhood* 100 (5): 482–88. https://www.ncbi.nlm.nih.gov/pmc/articles/PMC4413834/pdf/archdischild-2014-308114.pdf	Issues and criteria for application of neurodevelopmental assessment instruments in low-resource settings
Semrud-Clikeman, M., R. A. Romero, E. L. Prado, E. G. Shapiro, P. Bangirana, and C. C. John. 2017. "Selecting Measures for the Neurodevelopmental Assessment of Children in Low- and Middle-Income Countries." *Child Neuropsychology* 23 (7): 761–802. https://www.ncbi.nlm.nih.gov/pmc/articles/PMC5690490/	Issues and criteria for application of neurodevelopmental assessment instruments in low-resource settings
Cardiovascular disease	
Cosselman, K. E., A. Navas-Acien, and J. D. Kaufman. 2015. "Environmental Factors in Cardiovascular Disease." *Nature Reviews Cardiology* 12 (11): 627–42. https://www.nature.com/articles/nrcardio.2015.152	Discussion of lead (Pb), cadmium (Cd), arsenic (As), and cardiovascular disease
Mordukhovich, I., R. O. Wright, H. Hu, C. Amarasiriwardena, A. Baccarelli, A. Litonjua, D. Sparrow, P. Vokonas, and J. Schwartz. 2012. "Associations of Toenail Arsenic, Cadmium, Mercury, Manganese, and Lead with Blood Pressure in the Normative Aging Study." *Environmental Health Perspectives* 120 (1): 98–104. https://www.ncbi.nlm.nih.gov/pmc/articles/PMC3261928/	Observed associations between blood pressure and arsenic (As) and manganese but not the other metals

Bibliography

The "Health Outcomes" section of this bibliography lists studies of exposures to metals in relation to health outcomes as well as studies that discuss measurement of outcomes. Subsequent sections focus on studies relevant to artisanal small-scale gold mining (ASGM) and peer-reviewed literature on measurement methods and analysis of metals, particularly in terms of bioaccessibility and bioavailability.

HEALTH OUTCOMES

Barnett-Itzhaki, Z., M. E. López, N. Puttaswamy, and T. Berman. 2018. "A Review of Human Biomonitoring in Selected Southeast Asian Countries." *Environment international* 116: 156–64.

Bernard, A. 2008. "Biomarkers of Metal Toxicity in Population Studies: Research Potential and Interpretation Issues." *Journal of Toxicology and Environmental Health, Part A* 71 (18): 1259–65.

Boerma, J. T., E. Holt, and R. Black. 2001. "Measurement of Biomarkers in Surveys in Developing Countries: Opportunities and Problems." *Population and Development Review* 27 (2): 303–14.

Brindle, E., M. Fujita, J. Shofer, and K. A. O'Connor. 2010. "Serum, Plasma, and Dried Blood Spot High-Sensitivity C-Reactive Protein Enzyme Immunoassay for Population Research." *Journal of Immunological Methods* 362 (1–2): 112–20.

Crimmins, E., J. K. Kim, H. McCreath, J. Faul, D. Weir, and T. Seeman. 2014. "Validation of Blood-Based Assays Using Dried Blood Spots for Use in Large Population Studies." *Biodemography and Social Biology* 60 (1): 38–48. doi:10.1080/19485565.2014.901885.

Crimmins, E. M., J. D. Faul, J. K. Kim, and D. R. Weir. 2017. "Documentation of Blood-Based Biomarkers in the 2014 Health and Retirement Study." Report, Survey Research Center, Institute for Social Research, University of Michigan, Ann Arbor.

Delahaye, L., B. Janssens, and C. Stove. 2017. "Alternative Sampling Strategies for the Assessment of Biomarkers of Exposure." *Current Opinion in Toxicology* 4: 43–51.

Ercal, N., H. Gurer-Orhan, and N. Aykin-Burns. 2001. "Toxic Metals and Oxidative Stress Part I: Mechanisms Involved in Metal-Induced Oxidative Damage." *Current Topics in Medicinal Chemistry* 1 (6): 529–39.

Esteban, M., and A. Castaño. 2009. "Non-Invasive Matrices in Human Biomonitoring: A Review." *Environment International* 35 (2): 438–49.

FDA and NIH (US Food and Drug Administration and National Institutes of Health). 2016. "BEST (Biomarkers, EndpointS, and other Tools) Resource." Glossary copublished by the FDA, Silver Spring, MD; and NIH, Bethesda, MD. https://www.ncbi.nlm.nih.gov/books/NBK326791/.

Freeman, J. D., L. M. Rosman, J. D. Ratcliff, P. T. Strickland, D. R. Graham, and E. K. Silbergeld. 2017. "State of the Science in Dried Blood Spots." *Clinical Chemistry* 64 (4): 656–79. doi:10.1373/clinchem.2017.275966.

Funk, W. E., J. D. Pleil, D. J. Sauter, T. McDade, and J. L. Holl. 2015. "Use of Dried Blood Spots for Estimating Children's Exposures to Heavy Metals in Epidemiological Research." *Journal of Environmental & Analytical Toxicology* S7 (2): 1–9.

Garland, M., J. S. Morris, B. A. Rosner, M. J. Stampfer, V. L. Spate, C. J. Baskett, W. C. Willett, and D. J. Hunter. 1993. "Toenail Trace Element Levels as Biomarkers: Reproducibility Over a 6-Year Period." *Cancer Epidemiology and Prevention Biomarkers* 2 (5): 493–97.

Garrett, D. A., J. K. Sangha, M. T. Kothari, and D. Boyle. 2011. "Field-Friendly Techniques for Assessment of Biomarkers of Nutrition for Development." *American Journal of Clinical Nutrition* 94 (2): 685S–90S.

Holen, T., F. Norheim, T. E. Gundersen, P. Mitry, J. Linseisen, P. O. Iversen, and C. A. Drevon. 2016. "Biomarkers for Nutrient Intake with Focus on Alternative Sampling Techniques." *Genes & Nutrition* 11 (1): Article 12.

Jaszczak, A., K. Lundeen, and S. Smith. 2009. "Using Nonmedically Trained Interviewers to Collect Biomeasures in a National In-Home Survey." *Field Methods* 21 (1): 26–48.

Kakkar, P., and F. N. Jaffery. 2005. "Biological Markers for Metal Toxicity." *Environmental Toxicology and Pharmacology* 19 (2): 335–49.

Lacher, D. A., L. E. Berman, T.-C. Chen, and K. S. Porter. 2013. "Comparison of Dried Blood Spot to Venous Methods for Hemoglobin A1c, Glucose, Total Cholesterol, High-Density Lipoprotein Cholesterol, and C-Reactive Protein." *Clinica Chimica Acta* 422: 54–58.

Langer, E. K., K. J. Johnson, M. M. Shafer, P. Gorski, J. Overdier, J. Musselman, and J. A. Ross. 2011. "Characterization of the Elemental Composition of Newborn Blood Spots Using Sector-Field Inductively Coupled Plasma-Mass Spectrometry." *Journal of Exposure Science and Environmental Epidemiology* 21 (4): 355–64.

McDade, T. W. 2014. "Development and Validation of Assay Protocols for Use with Dried Blood Spot Samples." *American Journal of Human Biology* 26 (1): 1–9.

McDade, T. W., S. Williams, and J. J. Snodgrass. 2007. "What a Drop Can Do: Dried Blood Spots as a Minimally Invasive Method for Integrating Biomarkers into Population-Based Research." *Demography* 44 (4): 899–925.

Mei, J. 2014. "Dried Blood Spot Sample Collection, Storage, and Transportation." In *Dried Blood Spots: Applications and Techniques*, edited by W. Li and M. S. Lee, 21–31. Hoboken, NJ: John Wiley & Sons.

Neufeld, L., A. García-Guerra, D. Sánchez-Francia, O. Newton-Sánchez, M. D. Ramírez-Villalobos, and J. Rivera-Dommarco. 2002. "Hemoglobin Measured by Hemocue and a Reference Method in Venous and Capillary Blood: A Validation Study." *Salud Pública de México* 44 (3): 219–27.

NRC (National Research Council). 2006. Human Biomonitoring for Environmental Chemicals. Washington, DC: National Academies Press.

Ostler, M. W., J. H. Porter, and O. M. Buxton. 2014. "Dried Blood Spot Collection of Health Biomarkers to Maximize Participation in Population Studies." *Journal of Visualized Experiments* 2014 (83): e50973.

Poblete-Naredo, I., and A. Albores. 2016. "Molecular Biomarkers to Assess Health Risks Due to Environmental Contaminants Exposure." *Biomédica* 36 (2): 309–35.

Samuelsson, L. B., M. H. Hall, S. McLean, J. H. Porter, L. Berkman, M. Marino, G. Sembajwe, T. W. McDade, and O. M. Buxton. 2015. "Validation of Biomarkers of CVD Risk from Dried Blood Spots in Community-Based Research: Methodologies and Study-Specific Serum Equivalencies." *Biodemography and Social Biology* 61 (3): 285–97.

Sanchis-Gomar, F., J. Cortell-Ballester, H. Pareja-Galeano, G. Banfi, and G. Lippi. 2013. "Hemoglobin Point-of-Care Testing: The HemoCue System." *Journal of Laboratory Automation* 18 (3): 198–205.

Sanders, A. P., S. K. Miller, V. Nguyen, J. B. Kotch, and R. C. Fry. 2014. "Toxic Metal Levels in Children Residing in a Smelting Craft Village in Vietnam: A Pilot Biomonitoring Study." *BMC Public Health* 14 (1): Article 114.

Schindler, Birgit Karin, Marta Esteban, Holger Martin Koch, Argelia Castano, Stephan Koslitz, Ana Cañas, Ludwine Casteleyn, Marike Kolossa-Gehring, Gerda Schwedler, Greet Schoeters, Elly Den Hond, Ovnair Sepai, Karen Exley, Louis Bloemen, Milena Horvat, Lisbeth E Knudsen, Anke Joas, Reinhard Joas, Pierre Biot, Dominique Aerts, Ana Lopez, Olga Huetos, Andromachi Katsonouri, Katja Maurer-Chronakis, Lucie Kasparova, Karel Vrbík, Peter Rudnai, Miklos Naray, Cedric Guignard, Marc E. Fischer, Danuta Ligocka, Beata Janasik, M. Fátima Reis, Sónia Namorado, Cristian Pop, Irina Dumitrascu, Katarina Halzlova, Eleonora Fabianova, Darja Mazej, Janja Snoj Tratnik, Marika Berglund, Bo A. Jönsson, Andrea Lehmann, Pierre Crettaz, Hanne Frederiksen, Flemming Nielsen, Helena McGrath, Ian Nesbitt, Koen De Cremer, Guido Vanermen, Gudrun Koppen, Michael Wilhelm, Kerstin Becker, and Jürgen Angerer. 2014. "The European COPHES/DEMOCOPHES Project: Towards Transnational Comparability and Reliability of Human Biomonitoring Results." *International Journal of Hygiene and Environmental Health* 217 (6): 653–61.

Smolders, R., E. Den Hond, G. Koppen, E. Govarts, H. Willems, L. Casteleyn, M. Kolossa-Gehring et al. 2015. "Interpreting Biomarker Data from the COPHES/DEMOCOPHES Twin Projects: Using External Exposure Data to Understand Biomarker Differences Among Countries." *Environmental Research* 141: 86–95.

Timmerman, P., S. White, Z. Cobb, R. de Vries, E. Thomas, and B. van Baar. 2013. "Update of the EBF Recommendation for the Use of DBS in Regulated Bioanalysis Integrating the Conclusions from the EBF DBS-Microsampling Consortium." *Bioanalysis* 5 (17): 2129–36.

Vimercati, L., A. Baldassarre, M. F. Gatti, T. Gagliardi, M. Serinelli, L. De Maria, A. Caputi, Angelica A Dirodi, Ida Galise, Francesco Cuccaro, and Giorgio Assennato. 2016. "Non-Occupational Exposure to Heavy Metals of the Residents of an Industrial Area and Biomonitoring." *Environmental Monitoring and Assessment* 188 (12): Article 673.

Vimercati, L., F. Cuccaro, M. Serinelli, L. Bisceglia, I. Galise, M. Conversano, S. Minerba, A. Mincuzzi, T. Martino, M. A. Storelli, T. Gagliardi, and G. Assennato. 2013. "Exposure Assessment to Heavy Metals in General Population in a Polluted Area through Biological Monitoring." *E3S Web of Conferences* 1: Article 40005.

Were, F. H., W. Njue, J. Murungi, and R. Wanjau. 2008. "Use of Human Nails as Bio-Indicators of Heavy Metals Environmental Exposure Among School Age Children in Kenya." *Science of the Total Environment* 393 (2–3): 376–84.

WHO (World Health Organization). 2015. "Human Biomonitoring: Facts and Figures." Report, WHO Regional Office for Europe, Copenhagen.

Anemia

Balarajan, Y., U. Ramakrishnan, E. Özaltin, A. H. Shankar, and S. V. Subramanian. 2012. "Anaemia in Low-Income and Middle-Income Countries." *The Lancet* 378 (9809): 2123–35.

Parker, M., Z. Han, E. Abu-Haydar, E. Matsiko, D. Iyakaremye, L. Tuyisenge, A. Magaret, and A. Lyambabaje. 2018. "An Evaluation of Hemoglobin Measurement Tools and Their Accuracy and Reliability When Screening for Child Anemia in Rwanda: A Randomized Study." *PLoS One* 13 (1): e0187663

Sanchis-Gomar, F., J. Cortell-Ballester, H. Pareja-Galeano, G. Banfi, and G. Lippi. 2013. "Hemoglobin Point-of-Care Testing: the HemoCue System." *Journal of Laboratory Automation* 18 (3): 198–205.

Sharman, A. 2000. "Anemia Testing in Population-Based Surveys: General Information and Guidelines for Country Monitors and Program Managers." Guidance publication for the MEASURE DHS+ project, ORC Macro, Calverton, MD.

Yang, X., N. Z. Piety, S. M. Vignes, M. S. Benton, J. Kanter, and S. S. Shevkoplyas. 2013. "Simple Paper-Based Test for Measuring Blood Hemoglobin Concentration in Resource-Limited Settings." *Clinical Chemistry* 59 (10): 1506–13.

Carcinogenic markers

Albertini, R. J., D. Anderson, G. R. Douglas, L. Hagmar, K. Hemminki, F. Merlo, A. T. Natarajan et al. 2000. "IPCS Guidelines for the Monitoring of Genotoxic Effects of Carcinogens in Humans." *Mutation Research/Reviews in Mutation Research* 463 (2): 111–72.

Bonassi, S., L. Hagmar, U. Strömberg, A. H. Montagud, H. Tinnerberg, A. Forni, P. Heikkilä, S. Wanders, P. Wilhardt, I. L. Hansteen, L. E. Knudsen, and H. Norppa. 2000. "Chromosomal Aberrations in Lymphocytes Predict Human Cancer Independently of Exposure to Carcinogens." *Cancer Research* 60 (6): 1619–25.

Bonassi, S., D. Ugolini, M. Kirsch-Volders, U. Strömberg, R. Vermeulen, and J. D. Tucker. 2005. "Human Population Studies with Cytogenetic Biomarkers: Review of the Literature and Future Prospectives." *Environmental and Molecular Mutagenesis* 45 (2–3): 258–70.

Bonassi, S., A. Znaor, M. Ceppi, C. Lando, W. P. Chang, N. Holland, M. Kirsch-Volders, Errol Zeiger, Sadayuki Ban, Roberto Barale, Maria Paola Bigatti, Claudia Bolognesi, Antonina Cebulska-Wasilewska, Eleonora Fabianova, Alexandra Fucic, Lars Hagmar, Gordana Joksic, Antonietta Martelli, Lucia Migliore, Ekaterina Mirkova, Maria Rosaria Scarfi, Andrea Zijno, Hannu Norppa, and Michael Fenech. 2007. "An Increased Micronucleus Frequency in Peripheral Blood Lymphocytes Predict the Risk of Cancer in Humans." *Carcinogenesis* 28 (3): 625–31.

Farmer, P. B., and R. Singh. 2008. "Use of DNA Adducts to Identify Human Health Risk from Exposure to Hazardous Environmental Pollutants: The Increasing Role of Mass Spectrometry in Assessing Biologically Effective Doses of Genotoxic Carcinogens." *Mutation Research / Reviews in Mutation Research* 659 (1): 68–76.

Fenech, M. 2007. "Cytokinesis-Block Micronucleus Cytome Assay." *Nature Protocols* 2 (5): 1084–104. Change per http://cmosshoptalk.com/2018/04/10/316-7-316-17-or-316-317 -chicago-style-for-number-ranges/

Fenech, M., and A. A. Morley. 1985. "Measurement of Micronuclei in Lymphocytes." *Mutation Research / Environmental Mutagenesis and Related Subjects* 147 (1–2): 29–36.

Hagmar, L., S. Bonassi, U. Strömberg, A. Brøgger, L. E. Knudsen, H. Norppa, and C. Reuterwall. 1998. "Chromosomal Aberrations in Lymphocytes Predict Human Cancer: A Report from the European Study Group on Cytogenetic Biomarkers and Health (ESCH)." *Cancer Research* 58 (18): 4117–21.

Cardiovascular

Ahn, J. S., S. Choi, S. H. Jang, H. J. Chang, J. H. Kim, K. B. Nahm, S. W. Oh, and E. Y. Choi. 2003. "Development of a Point-of-Care Assay System for High-Sensitivity C-Reactive Protein in Whole Blood." *Clinica Chimica Acta* 332 (1–2): 51–59.

Cosselman, K. E., A. Navas-Acien, and J. D. Kaufman. 2015. "Environmental Factors in Cardiovascular Disease." *Nature Reviews Cardiology* 12 (11): 627–42.

McDade, T. W., J. Burhop, and J. Dohnal. 2004. "High-Sensitivity Enzyme Immunoassay for C-Reactive Protein in Dried Blood Spots." *Clinical Chemistry* 50 (3): 652–54.

Mordukhovich, I., R. O Wright, H. Hu, C. Amarasiriwardena, A. Baccarelli, A. Litonjua, D. Sparrow, P. Vokonas, and J. Schwartz. 2012. "Associations of Toenail Arsenic, Cadmium, Mercury, Manganese, and Lead with Blood Pressure in the Normative Aging Study." *Environmental Health Perspectives* 120 (1): 98–104.

Ochoa-Martínez, Á. C., E. D. Cardona-Lozano, L. Carrizales-Yáñez, and I. N. Pérez-Maldonado. 2018. "Serum Concentrations of New Predictive Cardiovascular Disease Biomarkers in Mexican Women Exposed to Lead." *Archives of Environmental Contamination and Toxicology* 74 (2): 248–58.

Peña, M. S. B., and A. Rollins. 2017. "Environmental Exposures and Cardiovascular Disease: A Challenge for Health and Development in Low- and Middle-Income Countries." *Cardiology Clinics* 35 (1): 71–86.

Roberts, W. L., L. Moulton, T. C. Law, G. Farrow, M. Cooper-Anderson, J. Savory, and N. Rifai. 2001. "Evaluation of Nine Automated High-Sensitivity C-Reactive Protein Methods: Implications for Clinical and Epidemiological Applications. Part 2." *Clinical Chemistry* 47 (3): 418–25.

Epigenetics

Arita, A., and M. Costa. 2009. "Epigenetics in Metal Carcinogenesis: Nickel, Arsenic, Chromium and Cadmium." *Metallomics* 1 (3): 222–28.

Cheng, T. F., S. Choudhuri, and K. Muldoon-Jacobs. 2012. "Epigenetic Targets of Some Toxicologically Relevant Metals: A Review of the Literature." *Journal of Applied Toxicology* 32 (9): 643–53.

Ercal, N., H. Gurer-Orhan, and N. Aykin-Burns. 2001. "Toxic Metals and Oxidative Stress Part I: Mechanisms Involved in Metal-Induced Oxidative Damage." *Current Topics in Medicinal Chemistry* 1 (6): 529–39.

Fragou, D., A. Fragou, S. Kouidou, S. Njau, and L. Kovatsi. 2011. "Epigenetic Mechanisms in Metal Toxicity." *Toxicology Mechanisms and Methods* 21 (4): 343–52.

Martinez-Zamudio, R., and H. C. Ha. 2011. "Environmental Epigenetics in Metal Exposure." *Epigenetics* 6 (7): 820–27.

Ryu, H.-W., D. H. Lee, H.-R. Won, K. H. Kim, Y. J. Seong, and S. H. Kwon. 2015. "Influence of Toxicologically Relevant Metals on Human Epigenetic Regulation." *Toxicological Research* 31 (1): 1–9.

Fetal growth

Sabra, S., E. Malmqvist, A. Saborit, E. Gratacós, and M. D. Roig. 2017. "Heavy Metals Exposure Levels and their Correlation with Different Clinical Forms of Fetal Growth Restriction." *PLoS One* 12 (10): e0185645.

Lung and lung function

Higashimoto, Y., T. Iwata, M. Okada, H. Satoh, K. Fukuda, and Y. Tohda. 2009. "Serum Biomarkers as Predictors of Lung Function Decline in Chronic Obstructive Pulmonary Disease." *Respiratory Medicine* 103 (8): 1231–38.

Measuring neurodevelopmental outcomes

Abubakar, A., P. Holding, A. Van Baar, C. R. Newton, and F. J. van de Vijver. 2008. "Monitoring Psychomotor Development in a Resource Limited Setting: An Evaluation of the Kilifi Developmental Inventory." *Annals of Tropical Paediatrics* 28 (3): 217–26.

Ballot, D. E., T. Ramdin, D. Rakotsoane, F. Agaba, V. A. Davies, T. Chirwa, and P. A. Cooper. 2017. "Use of the Bayley Scales of Infant and Toddler Development, Third Edition, to Assess Developmental Outcome in Infants and Young Children in an Urban Setting in South Africa." *International Scholarly Research Notices* 2017 (2): Article 1631760.

Dramé, C., and C. J. Ferguson. 2019. "Measurements of Intelligence in Sub-Saharan Africa: Perspectives Gathered from Research in Mali." *Current Psychology* 38 (2): 110–16.

Ertem, I. O., D. G. Dogan, C. G. Gok, S. U. Kizilates, A. Caliskan, G. Atay, N. Vatandas, T. Karaaslan, S. G. Baskan, and D. V. Cicchetti. 2008. "A Guide for Monitoring Child Development in Low- and Middle-Income Countries." *Pediatrics* 121 (3): e581–89.

Fernald, L. C., E. Prado, P. Kariger, and A. Raikes. 2017. "A Toolkit for Measuring Early Childhood Development in Low and Middle-Income Countries." Prepared for the Strategic Impact Evaluation Fund, World Bank, Washington, DC. [Report comes with an Excel spreadsheet to help guide selection of the appropriate instrument out of 147 possible instruments.]

Gladstone, M. J., G. A. Lancaster, A. P. Jones, K. Maleta, E. Mtitimila, P. Ashorn, and R. L. Smyth. 2008. "Can Western Developmental Screening Tools be Modified for Use in a Rural Malawian Setting?" *Archives of Disease in Childhood* 93 (1): 23–29.

Gladstone, M., G. A. Lancaster, E. Umar, M. Nyirenda, E. Kayira, N. R. van den Broek, and R. L. Smyth. 2010. "The Malawi Developmental Assessment Tool (MDAT): The Creation, Validation, and Reliability of a Tool to Assess Child Development in Rural African Settings." *PLoS Medicine* 7 (5): e1000273.

Holding, P. A., H. G. Taylor, S. D. Kazungu, T. Mkala, J. Gona, B. Mwamuye, L. Mbonani, and J. Stevenson. 2004. "Assessing Cognitive Outcomes in a Rural African Population: Development of a Neuropsychological Battery in Kilifi District, Kenya." *Journal of the International Neuropsychological Society* 10 (2): 246–60.

Janus, M., and D. R. Offord. 2007. "Development and Psychometric Properties of the Early Development Instrument (EDI): A Measure of Children's School Readiness." *Canadian Journal of Behavioural Science* 39 (1): 1–22.

McCoy, D. C., M. M. Black, B. Daelmans, and T. Dua. 2016. "Measuring Development in Children from Birth to Age 3 at Population Level." *Early Childhood Matters* 125: 34–39.

McCoy, D. C., E. D. Peet, M. Ezzati, G. Danaei, M. M. Black, C. R. Sudfeld, W. Fawzi, and G. Fink. 2016. "Early Childhood Developmental Status in Low- and Middle-Income Countries: National, Regional, and Global Prevalence Estimates Using Predictive Modeling." *PLoS Medicine* 13 (6): e1002034.

McCoy, D. C., C. R. Sudfeld, D. C. Bellinger, A. Muhihi, G. Ashery, T. E. Weary, W. Fawzi, and G. Fink. 2017. "Development and Validation of an Early Childhood Development Scale for Use in Low-Resourced Settings." *Population Health Metrics* 15 (1): Article 3.

Oppong, S. 2017. "Contextualizing Psychological Testing in Ghana." *Psychology & Its Contexts* 8 (1): 3–17.

Sabanathan, S., B. Wills, and M. Gladstone. 2015. "Child Development Assessment Tools in Low-Income and Middle-Income Countries: How Can We Use Them More Appropriately?" *Archives of Disease in Childhood* 100 (5): 482–88.

Semrud-Clikeman, M., R. A. Romero, E. L. Prado, E. G. Shapiro, P. Bangirana, and C. C. John. 2017. "Selecting Measures for the Neurodevelopmental Assessment of Children in Low- and Middle-Income Countries." *Child Neuropsychology* 23 (7): 761–802.

Metals exposure

Arsenic

Abdul, K. S., S. S. Jayasinghe, E. P. Chandana, C. Jayasumana, and P. M. De Silva. 2015. "Arsenic and Human Health Effects: A Review." *Environmental Toxicology and Pharmacology* 40 (3): 828–46.

Adonis, M., V. Martinez, P. Marin, and L. Gil. 2005. "CYP1A1 and GSTM1 Genetic Polymorphisms in Lung Cancer Populations Exposed to Arsenic in Drinking Water." *Xenobiotica* 35 (5): 519–30.

Ahir, B. K., A. P. Sanders, J. E. Rager, and R. C. Fry. 2013. "Systems Biology and Birth Defects Prevention: Blockade of the Glucocorticoid Receptor Prevents Arsenic-Induced Birth Defects." *Environmental Health Perspectives* 121 (3): 332–38.

Alamolhodaei, N. S., K. Shirani, and G. Karimi. 2015. "Arsenic Cardiotoxicity: An Overview." *Environmental Toxicology and Pharmacology* 40 (3): 1005–14.

Andrade, V. M., M. L. Mateus, M. C. Batoréu, M. Aschner, and A. M. Dos Santos. 2015. "Lead, Arsenic, and Manganese Metal Mixture Exposures: Focus on Biomarkers of Effect." *Biological Trace Element Research* 166 (1): 13–23.

Arita, A., and M. Costa. 2009. "Epigenetics in Metal Carcinogenesis: Nickel, Arsenic, Chromium and Cadmium." *Metallomics* 1 (3): 222–28.

Arslan, B., M. B. Djamgoz, and E. Akün. 2016. "ARSENIC: A Review on Exposure Pathways, Accumulation, Mobility and Transmission into the Human Food Chain." *Reviews of Environmental Contamination and Toxicology* 243: 27–51.

Bailey, K., and R. C. Fry. 2014. "Long-Term Health Consequences of Prenatal Arsenic Exposure: Links to the Genome and the Epigenome." *Reviews on Environmental Health* 29 (1–2): 9–12.

Bailey, K. A., A. H. Smith, E. J. Tokar, J. H. Graziano, K.-W. Kim, P. Navasumrit, M. Ruchirawat, A. Thiantanawat, W. A. Suk, and R. C. Fry. 2016. "Mechanisms Underlying Latent Disease Risk Associated with Early-Life Arsenic Exposure: Current Research Trends and Scientific Gaps." *Environmental Health Perspectives* 124 (2): 170–75.

Brender, J. D., L. Suarez, M. Felkner, Z. Gilani, D. Stinchcomb, K. Moody, J. Henry, and K. Hendricks. 2006. "Maternal Exposure to Arsenic, Cadmium, Lead, and Mercury and Neural Tube Defects in Offspring." *Environmental Research* 101 (1): 132–29.

Cubadda, F., B. P. Jackson, K. L. Cottingham, Y. O. Van Horne, and M. Kurzius-Spencer. 2017. "Human Exposure to Dietary Inorganic Arsenic and Other Arsenic Species: State of Knowledge, Gaps and Uncertainties." *Science of the Total Environment* 579: 1228–39.

de Burbure, C. D., J.-P. Buchet, A. Bernard, A. Leroyer, C. Nisse, J.-M. Haguenoer, E. Bergamaschi, and A. Mutti. 2003. "Biomarkers of Renal Effects in Children and Adults with Low Environmental Exposure to Heavy Metals." *Journal of Toxicology and Environmental Health Part A* 66 (9): 783–98.

de Burbure, C., J.-P. Buchet, A. Leroyer, C. Nisse, J.-M. Haguenoer, A. Mutti, Z. Smerhovský, Miroslav Cikrt, Malgorzata Trzcinka-Ochocka, Grazyna Razniewska, Marek Jakubowski, and Alfred Bernard. 2006. "Renal and Neurologic Effects of Cadmium, Lead, Mercury, and Arsenic in Children: Evidence of Early Effects and Multiple Interactions at Environmental Exposure Levels." *Environmental Health Perspectives* 114 (4): 584–90.

de la Calle, M. B., V. Devesa, Y. Fiamegos, and D. Vélez. 2017. "Determination of Inorganic Arsenic in a Wide Range of Food Matrices using Hydride Generation—Atomic Absorption Spectrometry." *Journal of Visualized Experiments* 2017 (127): e55953. doi:10.3791/55953.

DeSesso, J., C. Jacobson, A. Scialli, C. Farr, and J. Holson. 1998. "An Assessment of the Developmental Toxicity of Inorganic Arsenic." *Reproductive Toxicology* 12 (4): 385–433.

Fiamegkos, I., F. Cordeiro, P. Robouch, D. Vélez, V. Devesa, G. Raber, J. J. Sloth, R. R. Rasmussen, T. Llorente-Mirandes, J. F. Lopez-Sanchez, R. Rubio, F. Cubadda, M. D'Amato, J. Feldmann, A. Raab, H. Emteborg, and M. B. de la Callea. 2016. "Accuracy of a Method Based on Atomic Absorption Spectrometry to Determine Inorganic Arsenic in Food: Outcome of the Collaborative Trial IMEP-41." *Food Chemistry* 213: 169–79.

Flora, S. J., and S. Agrawal. 2017. "Arsenic, Cadmium, and Lead." In *Reproductive and Developmental Toxicology* 2nd ed., edited by R. C. Gupta, 537–66. London: Academic Press, an imprint of Elsevier.

Gamboa-Loira, B., M. E. Cebrián, F. Franco-Marina, and L. López-Carrillo. 2017. "Arsenic Metabolism and Cancer Risk: A Meta-Analysis." *Environmental Research* 156: 551–58.

Golub, M. S., M. S. Macintosh, and N. Baumrind. 1998. "Developmental and Reproductive Toxicity of Inorganic Arsenic: Animal Studies and Human Concerns." *Journal of Toxicology and Environmental Health, Part B Critical Reviews* 1 (3): 199–237.

Grau-Pérez, M., C.-C. Kuo, M. Spratlen, K. A. Thayer, M. A. Mendez, R. F. Hamman, D. Dabelea, John L. Adgate, William C. Knowler, Ronny A. Bell, Frederick W. Miller, Angela D. Liese, Chongben Zhang, Christelle Douillet, Zuzana Drobná, Elizabeth J. Mayer-Davis, Miroslav Stýblo, and Ana Navas-Acien. 2017. "The Association of Arsenic Exposure and Metabolism with Type 1 and Type 2 Diabetes in Youth: The SEARCH Case-Control Study." *Diabetes Care* 40 (1): 46–53.

Hata, A., H. Kurosawa, Y. Endo, K. Yamanaka, N. Fujitani, and G. Endo. 2010. "A Biological Indicator of Inorganic Arsenic Exposure Using the Sum of Urinary Inorganic Arsenic and Monomethylarsonic Acid Concentrations." *Journal of Occupational Health* 58 (2): 196–200.

Hays, S. M., L. L. Aylward, M. Gagné, A. Nong, and K. Krishnan. 2010. "Biomonitoring Equivalents for Inorganic Arsenic." *Regulatory Toxicology and Pharmacology* 58 (1): 1–9.

Jansen, R. J., M. Argos, L. Tong, J. Li, M. Rakibuz-Zaman, M. T. Islam, V. Slavkovich, Alauddin Ahmed, Ana Navas-Acien, Faruque Parvez, Yu Chen, Mary V. Gamble, Joseph H. Graziano, Brandon L. Pierce, and Habibul Ahsan. 2015. "Determinants and Consequences of Arsenic Metabolism Efficiency among 4,794 Individuals: Demographics, Lifestyle, Genetics, and Toxicity." *Cancer Epidemiology and Prevention Biomarkers* 25 (2): 381–90.

Jones, M. R., M. Tellez-Plaza, D. Vaidya, M. Grau, K. A. Francesconi, W. Goessler, E. Guallar, W. S. Post, J. D. Kaufman, and A. Navas-Acien. 2016. "Estimation of Inorganic Arsenic Exposure in Populations with Frequent Seafood Intake: Evidence From MESA and NHANES." *American Journal of Epidemiology* 184 (8): 590–602.

Kadono, T., T. Inaoka, N. Murayama, K. Ushijima, M. Nagano, S. Nakamura, C. Watanabe, K. Tamaki, and R. Ohtsuka. 2002. "Skin Manifestations of Arsenicosis in Two Villages in Bangladesh." *International Journal of Dermatology* 41 (12): 841–46.

Karagas, M. R., C. X. Le, S. T. Morris, J. O. Blum, X. I. Lu, V. I. Spate, M. A. Carey, V. I. Stannard, B. J. Klaue, and T. D. Tosteson. 2001. "Markers of Low Level Arsenic Exposure for Evaluating Human Cancer Risks in a US Population." *International Journal of Occupational Medicine and Environmental Health* 14 (2): 171–75.

Karagas, M. R., T. D. Tosteson, J. S. Morris, E. Demidenko, L. A. Mott, J. Heaney, and A. Schned. 2004. "Incidence of Transitional Cell Carcinoma of the Bladder and Arsenic Exposure in New Hampshire." *Cancer Causes & Control* 15 (5): 465–72.

Kuo, C-C., K. A. Moon, S. L. Wang, E. Silbergeld, and A. Navas-Acien. 2017. "The Association of Arsenic Metabolism with Cancer, Cardiovascular Disease, and Diabetes: A Systematic Review of the Epidemiological Evidence." *Environmental Health Perspectives* 125 (8): 087001.

Liu, L., J. R. Trimarchi, P. Navarro, M. A. Blasco, and D. L. Keefe. 2003. "Oxidative Stress Contributes to Arsenic-Induced Telomere Attrition, Chromosome Instability, and Apoptosis." *Journal of Biological Chemistry* 278 (34): 31998–2004.

Lynch, H. N., G. I. Greenberg, M. C. Pollock, and A. S. Lewis. 2014. "A Comprehensive Evaluation of Inorganic Arsenic in Food and Considerations for Dietary Intake Analyses." *Science of the Total Environment* 496: 299–313.

Marchiset-Ferlay, N., C. Savanovitch, and M. P. Sauvant-Rochat. 2012. "What Is the Best Biomarker to Assess Arsenic Exposure via Drinking Water?" *Environment International* 39 (1): 150–71.

Martinez, V. D., E. A. Vucic, D. D. Becker-Santos, L. Gil, and W. L. Lam. 2011. "Arsenic Exposure and the Induction of Human Cancers." *Journal of Toxicology* 2011 (5576): 431287.

Martínez-Sánchez, M. J., S. Martínez-López, L. B. Martínez-Martínez, and C. Pérez-Sirvent. 2013. "Importance of the Oral Arsenic Bioaccessibility Factor for Characterising the Risk Associated with Soil Ingestion in a Mining-Influenced Zone." *Journal of Environmental Management* 116: 10–17.

Michaud, D. S., M. E. Wright, K. P. Cantor, P. R. Taylor, J. Virtamo, and D. Albanes. 2004. "Arsenic Concentrations in Prediagnostic Toenails and the Risk of Bladder Cancer in a Cohort Study of Male Smokers." *American Journal of Epidemiology* 160 (9): 853–39. [no association]

Minatel, B. C., A. P. Sage, C. Anderson, R. Hubaux, E. A. Marshall, W. L. Lam, and V. D. Martinez. 2018. "Environmental Arsenic Exposure: From Genetic Susceptibility to Pathogenesis." *Environment International* 112: 183–97.

Naujokas, M. F., B. Anderson, H. Ahsan, H. V. Aposhian, J. H. Graziano, C. Thompson, and W. A. Suk. 2013. "The Broad Scope of Health Effects from Chronic Arsenic Exposure: Update on a Worldwide Public Health Problem." *Environmental Health Perspectives* 121 (3): 295–302.

Navas-Acien, A., E. K. Silbergeld, R. A. Streeter, J. M. Clark, T. A. Burke, and E. Guallar. 2006. "Arsenic Exposure and Type 2 Diabetes: A Systematic Review of the Experimental and Epidemiologic Evidence." *Environmental Health Perspectives* 114 (5): 641–48.

Nordberg, G. F., T. Jin, F. Hong, A. Zhang, F. P. Buchet, and B. Bernard. 2005. "Biomarkers of Cadmium and Arsenic Interactions." *Toxicology and Applied Pharmacology* 206 (2): 191–97.

Putila, J. J., and N. L. Guo. 2011. "Association of Arsenic Exposure with Lung Cancer Incidence Rates in the United States." *PLoS One* 6 (10): e25886.

Rasheed, H., R. Slack, and P. Kay. 2016. "Human Health Risk Assessment for Arsenic: A Critical Review." *Critical Reviews in Environmental Science and Technology* 46 (19–20): 1529–83.

Ray, P. D., A. Yosim, and R. C. Fry. 2014. "Incorporating Epigenetic Data into the Risk Assessment Process for the Toxic Metals Arsenic, Cadmium, Chromium, Lead, and Mercury: Strategies and Challenges." *Frontiers in Genetics* 5: Article 201.

Ren, X., C. M. McHale, C. F. Skibola, A. H. Smith, M. T. Smith, and L. Zhang. 2011. "An Emerging Role for Epigenetic Dysregulation in Arsenic Toxicity and Carcinogenesis." *Environmental Health Perspectives* 119 (1): 11–19.

Sanchez, T. R., M. Perzanowski, and J. H. Graziano. 2016. "Inorganic Arsenic and Respiratory Health, from Early Life Exposure to Sex-Specific Effects: A Systematic Review." *Environmental Research* 147: 537–55.

Shalat, S. L., D. B. Walker, and R. H. Finnell. 1996. "Role of Arsenic as a Reproductive Toxin with Particular Attention to Neural Tube Defects." *Journal of Toxicology and Environmental Health* 48 (3): 253–72.

Shen, H., Q. Niu, M. Xu, D. Rui, S. Xu, G. Feng, Y. Ding, S. Li, and M. Jing. 2016. "Factors Affecting Arsenic Methylation in Arsenic-Exposed Humans: A Systematic Review and Meta-Analysis." *International Journal of Environmental Research and Public Health* 13 (2): Article 205.

Smith, A. H., and C. M. Steinmaus. 2009. "Health Effects of Arsenic and Chromium in Drinking Water: Recent Human Findings." *Annual Review of Public Health* 2009 (30): 107–22.

Spratlen, M. J., M. V. Gamble, M. Grau-Perez, C.-C. Kuo, L. G. Best, J. Yracheta, K. Francesconi, Walter Goessler, Yasmin Mossavar-Rahmani, Meghan Hall, Jason G. Umans, Amanda Fretts, and Ana Navas-Acien. 2017. "Arsenic Metabolism and One-Carbon Metabolism at Low-Moderate Arsenic Exposure: Evidence from the Strong Heart Study." *Food and Chemical Toxicology* 105: 387–97.

Tolins, M., M. Ruchirawat, and P. Landrigan. 2014. "The Developmental Neurotoxicity of Arsenic: Cognitive and Behavioral Consequences of Early Life Exposure." *Annals of Global Health* 80 (4): 303–14.

Vahter, M. E. 2007. "Interactions between Arsenic-Induced Toxicity and Nutrition in Early Life." *Journal of Nutrition* 137 (12): 2798–804.

Vahter, M. 2008. "Health Effects of Early Life Exposure to Arsenic." *Basic & Clinical Pharmacology & Toxicology* 102 (2): 204–11.

Vahter, M. 2009. "Effects of Arsenic on Maternal and Fetal Health." *Annual Review of Nutrition* 29 (1): 381–99.

von Ehrenstein, O. S., S. Poddar, Y. Yuan, D. G. Mazumder, B. Eskenazi, A. Basu, M. Hira-Smith, Nalima Ghosh, Sabari Lahiri, Reina Haque, Alakendu Ghosh, Dave Kalman, Subankar Das, and Allan H. Smith. 2007. "Children's Intellectual Function in Relation to Arsenic Exposure." *Epidemiology* 18 (1): 44–51.

Wang, G., and B. A. Fowler. 2008. "Roles of Biomarkers in Evaluating Interactions among Mixtures of Lead, Cadmium and Arsenic." *Toxicology and Applied Pharmacology* 233 (1): 92–99.

Weidemann, D., C.-C. Kuo, A. Navas-Acien, A. G. Abraham, V. Weaver, and J. Fadrowski. 2015. "Association of Arsenic with Kidney Function in Adolescents and Young Adults: Results from the National Health and Nutrition Examination Survey 2009–2012." *Environmental Research* 140: 317–24.

Yager, J. W., T. Greene, and R. A. Schoof. 2015. "Arsenic Relative Bioavailability from Diet and Airborne Exposures: Implications for Risk Assessment." *Science of the Total Environment* 536: 368–81.

Lead

Aboh, I. J., M. A. Sampson, L. A. Nyaab, J. Caravanos, F. G. Ofosu, and H. Kuranchie-Mensah. 2013. "Assessing Levels of Lead Contamination in Soil and Predicting Pediatric Blood Lead Levels in Tema, Ghana." *Journal of Health and Pollution* 3 (5): 7–12.

Andrade, V. M., M. L. Mateus, M. C. Batoréu, M. Aschner, and A. M. Dos Santos. 2015. "Lead, Arsenic, and Manganese Metal Mixture Exposures: Focus on Biomarkers of Effect." *Biological Trace Element Research* 166 (1): 13–23.

Barbosa, F. Jr., J. E. Tanus-Santos, R. F. Gerlach, and P. J. Parsons. 2005. "A Critical Review of Biomarkers Used for Monitoring Human Exposure to Lead: Advantages, Limitations, and Future Needs." *Environmental Health Perspectives* 113 (12): 1669–74.

Binstock, D. A., W. F. Gutknecht, and A. C. McWilliams. 2009. "Lead in Soil—An Examination of Paired XRF Analysis Performed in the Field and Laboratory ICP-AES Results." *International Journal of Soil, Sediment and Water* 2 (2): Article 1.

Brender, J. D., L. Suarez, M. Felkner, Z. Gilani, D. Stinchcomb, K. Moody, J. Henry, and K. Hendricks. 2006. "Maternal Exposure to Arsenic, Cadmium, Lead, and Mercury and Neural Tube Defects in Offspring." *Environmental Research* 101 (1): 132–39.

Daniell, W. E., L. Van Tung, R. M. Wallace, D. J. Havens, C. J. Karr, N. Bich Diep, G. A. Croteau, N. J. Beaudet, and N. Duy Bao. 2015. "Childhood Lead Exposure from Battery Recycling in Vietnam." *BioMed Research International* 2015 (9): 193715.

de Burbure, C. D., J.-P. Buchet, A. Bernard, A. Leroyer, C. Nisse, J.-M. Haguenoer, E. Bergamaschi, and A. Mutti. 2003. "Biomarkers of Renal Effects in Children and Adults with Low Environmental Exposure to Heavy Metals." *Journal of Toxicology and Environmental Health Part A* 66 (9): 783–98.

de Burbure, C., J.-P. Buchet, A. Leroyer, C. Nisse, J.-M. Haguenoer, A. Mutti, Z. Smerhovský, Miroslav Cikrt, Malgorzata Trzcinka-Ochocka, Grazyna Razniewska, Marek Jakubowski, and Alfred Bernard. 2006. "Renal and Neurologic Effects of Cadmium, Lead, Mercury, and Arsenic in Children: Evidence of Early Effects and Multiple Interactions at Environmental Exposure Levels." *Environmental Health Perspectives* 114 (4): 584–90.

De Zwart, L. L., B. Klinck, and J. Van Wijnen. 2007. "Comparison of Five *In Vitro* Digestion Models to *In Vivo* Experimental Results: Lead Bioaccessibility in the Human Gastrointestinal Tract." *Journal of Environmental Science and Health Part A* 42 (9): 1203–11.

Ekong, E. B., B. G. Jaar, and V. M. Weaver. 2006. "Lead-Related Nephrotoxicity: A Review of the Epidemiologic Evidence." *Kidney international* 70 (12): 2074–84.

Ericson, B., P. P. Landrigan, M. P. Taylor, J. Frostad, J. Caravanos, J. Keith, and R. Fuller. 2016. "The Global Burden of Lead Toxicity Attributable to Informal Used Lead-Acid Battery Sites." *Annals of Global Health* 82 (5): 686–99.

Flora, S. J., and S. Agrawal. "Arsenic, Cadmium, and Lead." 2017. In *Reproductive and Developmental Toxicology*, 2nd ed., edited by R. C. Gupta, 537–66. London: Academic Press, an imprint of Elsevier.

Hambach, R., D. Lison, P. C. D'Haese, J. Weyler, E. De Graef, A. De Schryver, L. V. Lamberts, and M. Van Sprundel. 2013. "Co-Exposure to Lead Increases the Renal Response to Low Levels of Cadmium in Metallurgy Workers." *Toxicology Letters* 222 (2): 233–38.

Haryanto, B. 2016. "Lead Exposure from Battery Recycling in Indonesia." *Reviews on Environmental Health* 31 (1): 13–16.

Kummrow, F., F. F. Silva, R. Kuno, A. L. Souza, and P. V. Oliveira. 2008. "Biomonitoring Method for the Simultaneous Determination of Cadmium and Lead in Whole Blood by Electrothermal Atomic Absorption Spectrometry for Assessment of Environmental Exposure." *Talanta* 75 (1): 246–52.

Marschner, B., P. Welge, A. Hack, J. Wittsiepe, and M. Wilhelm. 2006. "Comparison of Soil Pb *In Vitro* Bioaccessibility and *In Vivo* Bioavailability with Pb Pools from a Sequential Soil Extraction." *Environmental Science & Technology* 40 (8): 2812–18.

Navas-Acien, A., E. Guallar, E. K. Silbergeld, and S. J. Rothenberg. 2007. "Lead Exposure and Cardiovascular Disease—A Systematic Review." *Environmental Health Perspectives* 115 (3): 472–82.

Nawrot, T. S., L. Thijs, E. M. Den Hond, H. A. Roels, and J. A. Staessen. 2002. "An Epidemiological Re-Appraisal of the Association between Blood Pressure and Blood Lead: A Meta-Analysis." *Journal of Human Hypertension* 16 (2): 123–31.

Ondayo, M. A., G. M. Simiyu, P. O. Raburu, and F. H. Were. 2016. "Child Exposure to Lead in the Vicinities of Informal Used Lead-Acid Battery Recycling Operations in Nairobi Slums, Kenya." *Journal of Health and Pollution* 6 (12): 15–25.

Ray, P. D., A. Yosim, and R. C. Fry. 2014. "Incorporating Epigenetic Data into the Risk Assessment Process for the Toxic Metals Arsenic, Cadmium, Chromium, Lead, and Mercury: Strategies and Challenges." *Frontiers in Genetics* 5: Article 201.

Sanders, T., Y. Liu, V. Buchner, and P. B. Tchounwou. 2009. "Neurotoxic Effects and Biomarkers of Lead Exposure: A Review." *Reviews on Environmental Health* 24 (1): 15–46.

Tsaih, S.-W., S. Korrick, J. Schwartz, C. Amarasiriwardena, A. Aro, D. Sparrow, and H. Hu. 2004. "Lead, Diabetes, Hypertension, and Renal Function: The Normative Aging Study." *Environmental Health Perspectives* 112 (11): 1178–82.

Wang, G., and B. A. Fowler. 2008. "Roles of Biomarkers in Evaluating Interactions among Mixtures of Lead, Cadmium and Arsenic." *Toxicology and Applied Pharmacology* 233 (1): 92–99.

Zahran, S., M. A. Laidlaw, S. P. McElmurry, G. M. Filippelli, and M. Taylor. 2013. "Linking Source and Effect: Resuspended Soil Lead, Air Lead, and Children's Blood Lead Levels in Detroit, Michigan." *Environmental Science & Technology* 47 (6): 2839–45.

Zia, M. H., E. E. Codling, K. G. Scheckel, and R. L. Chaney. 2011. "*In Vitro* and *In Vivo* Approaches for the Measurement of Oral Bioavailability of Lead (Pb) in Contaminated Soils: A Review." *Environmental Pollution* 159 (10): 2320–27.

Mercury and Methylmercury

Baeuml, J., S. Bose-O'Reilly, R. M. Gothe, B. Lettmeier, G. Roider, G. Drasch, and U. Siebert. 2011. "Human Biomonitoring Data from Mercury Exposed Miners in Six Artisanal Small-Scale Gold Mining Areas in Asia and Africa." *Minerals* 1 (1): 122–43.

Baeuml, J., S. Bose-O'Reilly, B. Lettmeier, A. Maydl, K. Messerer, G. Roider, G. Drasch, and U. Siebert. 2011. "Applicability of Two Mobile Analysers for Mercury in Urine in Small-Scale Gold Mining Areas." *International Journal of Hygiene and Environmental Health* 215 (1): 64–67.

Basu, N., J. M. Goodrich, and J. Head. 2014. "Ecogenetics of Mercury: From Genetic Polymorphisms and Epigenetics to Risk Assessment and Decision-Making." *Environmental Toxicology and Chemistry* 33 (6): 1248–58.

Berglund, M., B. Lind, K. A. Björnberg, B. Palm, Ö. Einarsso, and M. Vahter. 2005. "Inter-Individual Variations of Human Mercury Exposure Biomarkers: A Cross-Sectional Assessment." *Environmental Health* 4 (1): Article 20.

Bose-O'Reilly, S., K. M. McCarty, N. Steckling, and B. Lettmeier. 2010. "Mercury Exposure and Children's Health." *Current Problems in Pediatric and Adolescent Health Care* 40 (8): 186–215.

Brender, J. D., L. Suarez, M. Felkner, Z. Gilani, D. Stinchcomb, K. Moody, J. Henry, and K. Hendricks. 2006. "Maternal Exposure to Arsenic, Cadmium, Lead, and Mercury and Neural Tube Defects in Offspring." *Environmental Research* 101 (1): 132–39.

Cardenas, A., S. L. Rifas-Shiman, G. Agha, M.-F. Hivert, A. A. Litonjua, D. L. DeMeo, X. Lin, Chitra Amarasiriwardena, Emily Oken, Matthew W. Gillman, and Andrea A. Baccarelli. 2017. "Persistent DNA Methylation Changes Associated with Prenatal Mercury Exposure and Cognitive Performance during Childhood." *Scientific Reports* 7 (1): Article 288.

de Burbure, C. D., J.-P. Buchet, A. Bernard, A. Leroyer, C. Nisse, J.-M. Haguenoer, E. Bergamaschi, and A. Mutti. 2003. "Biomarkers of Renal Effects in Children and Adults with Low Environmental Exposure to Heavy Metals." *Journal of Toxicology and Environmental Health Part A* 66 (9): 783–98.

de Burbure, C., J.-P. Buchet, A. Leroyer, C. Nisse, J.-M. Haguenoer, A. Mutti, Z. Smerhovský, M. Cikrt, M. Trzcinka-Ochocka, G. Razniewska, and M. Jakubowski. 2006. "Renal and Neurologic Effects of Cadmium, Lead, Mercury, and Arsenic in Children: Evidence of Early Effects and Multiple Interactions at Environmental Exposure Levels." *Environmental Health Perspectives* 114 (4): 584–90.

De Lacerda, L. 2003. "Updating Global Hg Emissions from Small-Scale Gold Mining and Assessing Its Environmental Impacts." *Environmental Geology* 43 (3): 308–14.

Doering, S., S. Bose-O'Reilly, and U. Berger. 2016. "Essential Indicators Identifying Chronic Inorganic Mercury Intoxication: Pooled Analysis across Multiple Cross-Sectional Studies." *PLoS One* 11 (8): e0160323.

dos Santos, A. A., M. A. Hort, M. Culbreth, C. López-Granero, M. Farina, J. B. Rocha, and M. Aschner. 2016. "Methylmercury and Brain Development: A Review of Recent Literature." *Journal of Trace Elements in Medicine and Biology* 38: 99–107.

Esteban, Marta, Birgit Karin Schindler, José Antonio Jiménez, Holger Martin Koch, Jürgen Angerer, Montserrat Rosado, Silvia Gómez, Ludwine Casteleyn, Marike Kolossa-Gehring, Kerstin Becker, Louis Bloemen, Greet Schoeters, Elly Den Hond, Ovnair Sepai, Karen Exley, Milena Horvat, Lisbeth E Knudsen, Anke Joas, Reinhard Joas, Dominique Aerts, Pierre Biot, Daniela Borošová, Fred Davidson, Irina Dumitrascu, Marc E. Fischer, Margaretha Grander, Beata Janasik, Kate Jones, Lucie Kašparová, Thorjørn Larssen, Miklos Naray, Flemming Nielsen, Philipp Hohenblum, Rui Pinto, Catherine Pirard, Gregory Plateel, Janja Snoj Tratnik, Jürgen Wittsiepe, Argelia Castaño, and EQUAS Reference Laboratories. 2015. "Mercury Analysis in Hair: Comparability and Quality Assessment within the Transnational COPHES/DEMOCOPHES Project." *Environmental Research* 141: 24–30.

Gibb, H., and K. G. O'Leary. 2014. "Mercury Exposure and Health Impacts among Individuals in the Artisanal and Small-Scale Gold Mining Community: A Comprehensive Review." *Environmental Health Perspectives* 122 (7): 667–72.

Gray, J. E., V. F. Labson, J. N. Weaver, and D. P. Krabbenhoft. 2002. "Mercury and Methylmercury Contamination Related to Artisanal Gold Mining, Suriname." *Geophysical Research Letters* 29 (23): Article 20.

Gustin, K., F. Tofail, F. Mehrin, M. Levi, M. Vahter, and M. Kippler. 2017. "Methylmercury Exposure and Cognitive Abilities and Behavior at 10 Years of Age." *Environment International* 102: 97–105.

Kristensen, A. K., J. F. Thomsen, and S. Mikkelsen. 2014. "A Review of Mercury Exposure among Artisanal Small-Scale Gold Miners in Developing Countries." *International Archives of Occupational and Environmental Health* 87 (6): 579–90.

Marques, R. C., J. V. Bernardi, L. Abreu, and J. G. Dórea. 2015. "Neurodevelopment Outcomes in Children Exposed to Organic Mercury from Multiple Sources in a Tin-Ore Mine Environment in Brazil." *Archives of Environmental Contamination and Toxicology* 68 (3): 432–41.

Rajaee, M., R. N. Long, E. P. Renne, and N. Basu. 2015. "Mercury Exposure Assessment and Spatial Distribution in a Ghanaian Small-Scale Gold Mining Community." *International Journal of Environmental Research and Public Health* 12 (9): 10755–82.

Ray, P. D., A. Yosim, and R. C. Fry. 2014. "Incorporating Epigenetic Data into the Risk Assessment Process for the Toxic Metals Arsenic, Cadmium, Chromium, Lead, and Mercury: Strategies and Challenges." *Frontiers in Genetics* 5: Article 201.

Sari, M. M., T. Inoue, Y. Matsumoto, and K. Yokota. 2016. "Measuring Total Mercury Due to Small-Scale Gold Mining Activities to Determine Community Vulnerability in Cihonje, Central Java, Indonesia." *Water Science and Technology* 73 (2): 437–44.

Sherman, L. S., J. D. Blum, N. Basu, M. Rajaee, D. C. Evers, D. G. Buck, J. Petrlik, and J. DiGangi. 2015. "Assessment of Mercury Exposure among Small-Scale Gold Miners Using Mercury Stable Isotopes." *Environmental Research* 137: 226–34.

Steckling, N., S. Boese-O'Reilly, C. Gradel, K. Gutschmidt, E. Shinee, E. Altangerel, B. Badrakh, Ichinkhorloo Bonduush, Unursaikhan Surenjav, Philip Ferstl, Gabriele Roider, Mineshi Sakamoto, Ovnair Sepai, Gustav Drasch, Beate Lettmeier, Jackie Morton, Kate Jones, Uwe Siebert, Claudia Hornberg. 2011. "Mercury Exposure in Female Artisanal Small-Scale Gold Miners (ASGM) on Mongolia: An Analysis of Human Biomonitoring (HBM) Data from 2008." *Science of the Total Environment* 409 (5): 994–1000.

Steckling, N., S. Bose-O'Reilly, P. Pinheiro, D. Plass, D. Shoko, G. Drasch, L. Bernaudat, U. Siebert, and C. Hornberg. 2014. "The Burden of Chronic Mercury Intoxication in Artisanal Small-Scale Gold Mining in Zimbabwe: Data Availability and Preliminary Estimates." *Environmental Health* 13 (1): Article 111.

Tschakert, P., and K. Singha. 2007. "Contaminated Identities: Mercury and Marginalization in Ghana's Artisanal Mining Sector." *Geoforum* 38 (6): 1304–21.

van Wijngaarden, E., S. W. Thurston, G. J. Myers, D. Harrington, D. A. Cory-Slechta, J. J. Strain, G. E. Watson, Grazyna Zareba, Tanzy Love, Juliette Henderson, Conrad F. Shamlaye, and Philip W. Davidson. 2017. "Methyl Mercury Exposure and Neurodevelopmental Outcomes in the Seychelles Child Development Study Main Cohort at Age 22 and 24 Years." *Neurotoxicology and Teratology* 59: 35–42.

Wyatt, L., E. J. Ortiz, B. Feingold, A. Berky, S. Diringer, A. M. Morales, E. R. Jurado, H. Hsu-Kim, and W. Pan. 2017. "Spatial, Temporal, and Dietary Variables Associated with Elevated Mercury Exposure in Peruvian Riverine Communities Upstream and Downstream of Artisanal and Small-Scale Gold Mining." *International Journal of Environmental Research and Public Health* 14 (12): Article 1582.

Renal outcomes

D'Amico, G., and C. Bazzi. 2003. "Urinary Protein and Enzyme Excretion as Markers of Tubular Damage." *Current Opinion in Nephrology and Hypertension* 12 (6): 639–43.

Earley, A., D. Miskulin, E. J. Lamb, A. S. Levey, and K. Uhlig. 2012. "Estimating Equations for Glomerular Filtration Rate in the Era of Creatinine Standardization." *Annals of Internal Medicine* 156 (11): 785–95.

Lamb, E. J., F. MacKenzie, and P. E. Stevens. 2009. "How Should Proteinuria Be Detected and Measured?" *Annals of Clinical Biochemistry* 46 (3): 205–17.

Levey, A. S., L. A. Stevens, C. H. Schmid, Y. L. Zhang, A. F. Castro, H. I. Feldman, J. W. Kusek, Paul Eggers, Frederick Van Lente, Tom Greene, and Josef Coresh. 2009. "A New Equation to Estimate Glomerular Filtration Rate." *Annals of Internal Medicine* 150 (9): 604–12.

Prigent, A. 2008. "Monitoring Renal Function and Limitations of Renal Function Tests." *Seminars in Nuclear Medicine* 38 (1): 32–46.

SBU (Swedish Council on Health Technology Assessment). 2013. "Methods to Estimate and Measure Renal Function (Glomerular Filtration Rate) A Systematic Review." Yellow Report No. 214, SBU, Stockholm. https://www.ncbi.nlm.nih.gov/pubmedhealth/PMH0078717 /pdf/PubMedHealth_PMH0078717.pdf.

Traynor, J., R. Mactier, C. C. Geddes, and J. G. Fox. 2006. "How to Measure Renal Function in Clinical Practice." *BMJ* 333 (7571): 733–37.

Weaver, V. M., D. J. Kotchmar, J. J. Fadrowski, and E. K. Silbergeld. 2016. "Challenges for Environmental Epidemiology Research: Are Biomarker Concentrations Altered by Kidney Function or Urine Concentration Adjustment?" *Journal of Exposure Science and Environmental Epidemiology* 26 (1): 1–8.

ASGM AND OTHER RELEVANT STUDIES

Ajumobi, O. O., A. Tsofo, M. Yango, M. K. Aworh, I. N. Anagbogu, A. Mohammed, N. Umar-Tsafe et al. 2014. "High Concentration of Blood Lead Levels Among Young Children in Bagega Community, Zamfara–Nigeria and the Potential Risk Factor." *Pan African Medical Journal* 18 (Suppl 1): Article 14.

Armah, F. A., and E. K. Gyeabour. 2013. "Health Risks to Children and Adults Residing in Riverine Environments Where Surficial Sediments Contain Metals Generated by Active Gold Mining in Ghana." *Toxicological Research* 29 (1): 69–79.

Armah, F. A., M. Kuitunen, I. Luginaah, and P. Mkandawire. 2012. "Non-Occupational Health Risk Assessment from Exposure to Chemical Contaminants in the Gold Mining Environment of Tarkwa, Ghana." *Trends in Applied Sciences Research* 7 (3): 181–95.

Armah, F. A., I. Luginaah, and S. Obiri. 2012. "Assessing Environmental Exposure and Health Impacts of Gold Mining in Ghana." *Toxicological & Environmental Chemistry* 94 (4): 786–98.

Armah, F. A., S. Obiri, D. O. Yawson, E. E. Onumah, G. T. Yengoh, E. K. Afrifa, and J. O. Odoi. 2010. "Anthropogenic Sources and Environmentally Relevant Concentrations of Heavy Metals in Surface Water of a Mining District in Ghana: A Multivariate Statistical Approach." *Journal of Environmental Science and Health Part A* 45 (13): 1804–13.

Basu, N., E. Clarke, A. Green, B. Calys-Tagoe, L. Chan, M. Dzodzomenyo, J. Fobil, Rachel N. Long, Richard L. Neitzel, Samuel Obiri, Eric Odei, Lauretta Ovadje, Reginald Quansah, Mozhgon Rajaee, and Mark L. Wilson. 2015. "Integrated Assessment of Artisanal And Small-Scale Gold Mining in Ghana—Part 1: Human Health Review." *International Journal of Environmental Research and Public Health* 12 (5): 5143–76.

Basu, N., E. P. Renne, and R. N. Long. 2015. "An Integrated Assessment Approach to Address Artisanal and Small-Scale Gold Mining in Ghana." *International Journal of Environmental Research and Public Health* 12 (9): 11683–98. https://www.ncbi.nlm.nih.gov/pmc/articles /PMC4586700/pdf/ijerph-12-11683.pdf

Bawa, I. 2010. "A Viewpoint on Small-Scale Gold Mining in Ghana: A Regulatory Perspective on Current Practices, Mercury Use and the UNIDO And EU Projects." *International Journal of Environment and Pollution* 41 (3–4): 195–201.

Bose-O'Reilly, S., G. Drasch, C. Beinhoff, S. Rodrigues-Filho, G. Roider, B. Lettmeier, A. Maydl, S. Maydl, and U. Siebert. 2010. "Health Assessment of Artisanal Gold Miners in Indonesia." *Science of the Total Environment* 408 (4): 713–25.

Bose-O'Reilly, S., G. Drasch, C. Beinhoff, A. Tesha, K. Drasch, G. Roider, H. Taylor, D. Appleton, and U. Siebert. 2010. "Health Assessment of Artisanal Gold Miners in Tanzania." *Science of the Total Environment* 408 (4): 796–805.

Caravanos, J., B. Ericson, J. Ponce-Canchihuamán, D. Hanrahan, M. Block, B. Susilorini, and R. Fuller. 2013. "Rapid Assessment of Environmental Health Risks Posed by Mining Operations in Low- and Middle-Income Countries: Selected Case Studies." *Environmental Science and Pollution Research* 20 (11): 7711–18.

Cobbina, S. J., A. B. Duwiejuah, R. Quansah, S. Obiri, and N. Bakobie. 2015. "Comparative Assessment of Heavy Metals in Drinking Water Sources in Two Small-Scale Mining Communities in Northern Ghana." *International Journal of Environmental Research and Public Health* 12 (9): 10620–34.

Cobbina, S. J., M. Myilla, and K. Michael. 2013. "Small-Scale Gold Mining and Heavy Metal Pollution: Assessment of Drinking Water Sources in Datuku in the Talensi-Nabdam District." *International Journal of Scientific & Technology Research* 2 (1): 96–100.

Dowling, R., B. Ericson, J. Caravanos, P. Grigsby, and Y. Amoyaw-Osei. 2015. "Spatial Associations between Contaminated Land and Socio Demographics in Ghana." *International Journal of Environmental Research and Public Health* 12 (10): 13587–601.

Dzomba, P., S. Nyoni, and N. Mudavanhu. 2012. "Heavy Metal Contamination Risk through Consumption of Traditional Food Plants Growing around Bindura Town, Zimbabwe." *Journal of Toxicology and Environmental Health Sciences* 4 (5): 92–95.

Ericson, B., J. Caravanos, K. Chatham-Stephens, P. Landrigan, and R. Fuller. 2013. "Approaches to Systematic Assessment of Environmental Exposures Posed at Hazardous Waste Sites in the Developing World: The Toxic Sites Identification Program." *Environmental Monitoring and Assessment* 185 (2): 1755–66.

Glorennec, P., J. P. Lucas, C. Mandin, and B. Le Bot. 2012. "French Children's Exposure to Metals via Ingestion of Indoor Dust, Outdoor Playground Dust and Soil: Contamination Data." *Environment International* 45 (1): 129–34.

Islam, M. S., M. K. Ahmed, and M. Habibullah-Al-Mamun. 2015. "Metal Speciation in Soil and Health Risk due to Vegetables Consumption in Bangladesh." *Environmental Monitoring and Assessment* 187 (5): Article 288.

Kamunda, C., M. Mathuthu, and M. Madhuku. 2018. "Potential Human Risk of Dissolved Heavy Metals in Gold Mine Waters of Gauteng Province, South Africa." *Journal of Toxicology and Environmental Health Sciences* 10 (6): 56–63.

Khan, M. U., R. N. Malik, and S. Muhammad. 2013. "Human Health Risk from Heavy Metal via Food Crops Consumption with Wastewater Irrigation Practices in Pakistan." *Chemosphere* 93 (10): 2230–38.

Langeland, A. L., R. D. Hardin, and R. L. Neitzel. 2017. "Mercury Levels in Human Hair and Farmed Fish Near Artisanal and Small-Scale Gold Mining Communities in the Madre de Dios River Basin, Peru." *International Journal of Environmental Research and Public Health* 14 (3): Article 302.

Mbilu, Z. J., and M. E. Lyimo. 2015. "Heavy Metals Contamination in Soils and Selected Edible Parts of Free-Range Local Chicken." *International Journal of Environmental Science and Technology* 12 (4): 1409–14.

Muhanji, G., R. L. Roothaert, C. Webo, and M. Stanley. 2011. "African Indigenous Vegetable Enterprises and Market Access for Small-Scale Farmers in East Africa." *International Journal of Agricultural Sustainability* 9 (1): 194–202.

Niane, B., S. Guédron, R. Moritz, C. Cosio, P. M. Ngom, N. Deverajan, H. R. Pfeifer, and J. Poté. 2015. "Human Exposure to Mercury in Artisanal Small-Scale Gold Mining Areas of Kedougou Region, Senegal, as a Function of Occupational Activity and Fish Consumption." *Environmental Science and Pollution Research* 22 (9): 7101–11.

O'Connor, D., D. Hou, Y. S. Ok, J. Mulder, L. Duan, Q. Wu, S. Wang, F. M. Tack, and J. Rinklebe. 2019. "Mercury Speciation, Transformation, and Transportation in Soils, Atmospheric Flux, and Implications for Risk Management: A Critical Review." *Environment International* 126 (9): 747–61.

Oguri, T., G. Suzuki, H. Matsukami, N. Uchida, N. M. Tue, P. H. Viet, S. Takahashi, S. Tanabe, and H. Takigami. 2018. "Exposure Assessment of Heavy Metals in an E-Waste Processing Area in Northern Vietnam." *Science of the Total Environment* 621: 1115–23.

Okoye, C. O., C. N. Ibeto, and J. N. Ihedioha. 2011. "Assessment of Heavy Metals in Chicken Feeds Sold in South Eastern, Nigeria." *Advances in Applied Science Research* 2 (3): 63–68.

Olowoyo, J. O., L. L. Mugivhisa, and Z. G. Magoloi. 2016. "Composition of Trace Metals in Dust Samples Collected from Selected High Schools in Pretoria, South Africa." *Applied and Environmental Soil Science* 2016: 5829657.

Olujimi, O. O., O. Oputu, O. Fatoki, O. E. Opatoyinbo, O. A. Aroyewun, and J. Baruani. 2015. "Heavy Metals Speciation and Human Health Risk Assessment at an Illegal Gold Mining Site in Igun, Osun State, Nigeria." *Journal of Health Pollution* 5 (8): 19–32.

Ouboter, P. E., G. Landburg, G. U. Satnarain, S. Y. Starke, I. Nanden, B. Simon-Friedt, W. B. Hawkins, R. Taylor, M. Y. Lichtveld, E. Harville, and J. K. Wickliffe. 2018. "Mercury Levels in Women and Children from Interior Villages in Suriname, South America." *International Journal of Environmental Research and Public Health* 15 (5): Article 1007.

Plumlee, G. S., J. T. Durant, S. A. Morman, A. Neri, R. E. Wolf, C. A. Dooyema, P. L. Hageman, Heather A. Lowers, Gregory L. Fernette, Gregory P. Meeker, William M. Benzel, Rhonda L. Driscoll, Cyrus J. Berry, James G. Crock, Harland L. Goldstein, Monique Adams, Casey L. Bartrem, Simba Tirima, Behrooz Behbod, Ian von Lindern, Mary Jean Brown. 2013. "Linking Geological and Health Sciences to Assess Childhood Lead Poisoning from Artisanal Gold Mining in Nigeria." *Environmental Health Perspectives* 121 (6): 744–50.

Rajaee, M., R. Long, E. Renne, and N. Basu. 2015. "Mercury Exposure Assessment and Spatial Distribution in a Ghanaian Small-Scale Gold Mining Community." *International Journal of Environmental Research and Public Health* 12 (9): 10755–82.

Rajaee, M., S. Obiri, A. Green, R. Long, S. J. CobbinaJ, V. Nartey, D. Buck, E. Antwi, and N. Basu. 2015. "Integrated Assessment of Artisanal and Small-Scale Gold Mining in Ghana—Part 2: Natural Sciences Review." *International Journal of Environmental Research and Public Health* 12 (8): 8971–9011.

Röllin, H. B., C. V. Rudge, Y. Thomassen, A. Mathee, and J. Ø. Odland. 2009. "Levels of Toxic and Essential Metals in Maternal and Umbilical Cord Blood from Selected Areas of South Africa—Results of a Pilot Study." *Journal of Environmental Monitoring* 11 (3): 618–27.

Taiwo, A. M., and J. A. Awomeso. 2017. "Assessment of Trace Metal Concentration and Health Risk of Artisanal Gold Mining Activities in Ijeshaland, Osun State Nigeria—Part 1." *Journal of Geochemical Exploration* 177: 1–10.

Tijjani, M. B., B. M. Agaie, K. I. Onifade, A. S. Mainasara, I. L. Yusuf, and A. O. Tijjani. 2019. "Post-Epidemic Lead Exposure to Animals following a Decontamination Exercise in Gold Mining Village of Bagega, Zamfara State, Nigeria." *Journal of Toxicology and Environmental Health Sciences* 11 (3): 32–37.

Tirima, S., C. Bartrem, I. von Lindern, M. von Braun, D. Lind, S. M. Anka, and A. Abdullahi. 2016. "Environmental Remediation to Address Childhood Lead Poisoning Epidemic due to Artisanal Gold Mining in Zamfara, Nigeria." *Environmental Health Perspectives* 124 (9): 1471–78.

Tirima, S., C. Bartrem, I. von Lindern, M. von Braun, D. Lind, S. M. Anka, and A. Abdullahi. 2018. "Food Contamination as a Pathway for Lead Exposure in Children during the 2010–2013 Lead Poisoning Epidemic in Zamfara, Nigeria." *Journal of Environmental Sciences* 67: 260–72.

Vega, C. M., J. D. Orellana, M. W. Oliveira, S. S. Hacon, and P. C. Basta. 2018. "Human Mercury Exposure in Yanomami Indigenous Villages from the Brazilian Amazon." *International Journal of Environmental Research and Public Health* 15 (6): Article 1051.

WHO, UNEP, and IOMC (World Health Organization, United Nations Environment Programme, and Inter-Organization Programme for the Sound Management of Chemicals). 2008. "Guidance for Identifying Populations at Risk from Mercury Exposure." Guide and reference document, WHO and UNEP, Geneva.

Wyatt, L., E. J. Ortiz, B. Feingold, A. Berky, S. Diringer, A. M. Morales, E. R. Jurado, H. Hsu-Kim, and W. Pan. 2017. "Spatial, Temporal, and Dietary Variables Associated with Elevated Mercury Exposure in Peruvian Riverine Communities Upstream and Downstream of Artisanal and Small-Scale Gold Mining." *International Journal of Environmental Research and Public Health* 14 (12): Article 1582.

Zheng, J., K.-H. Chen, X. Yan, S.-J. Chen, G.-C. Hu, X.-W. Peng, J.-G. Yuan, B.-X. Mai, and Z.-Y. Yang. 2013. "Heavy Metals in Food, House Dust, and Water from an E-Waste Recycling Area in South China and the Potential Risk to Human Health." *Ecotoxicology and Environmental Safety* 96: 205–12.

Zhuang, P., B. Zou, H. Lu, and Z. Li. 2014. "Heavy Metal Concentrations in Five Tissues of Chickens from a Mining Area." *Polish Journal of Environmental Studies* 23 (6): 2375–79.

METHODS

The sources listed here cover only the peer-reviewed literature (as opposed to guidance); bioaccessibility / bioavailability. For a complete official methods compilation, see "Hazardous Waste Methods / SW-846" (https://www.epa.gov /hw-sw846) and "Collection of Methods" (https://www.epa.gov /measurements-modeling/collection-methods) on the US Environmental Protection Agency (EPA) website.

Brent, R. N., H. Wines, J. Luther, N. Irving, J. Collins, and D. L. Drake. 2017. "Validation of Handheld X-Ray Fluorescence for *In Situ* Measurement of Mercury in Soils." *Journal of Environmental Chemical Engineering* 5 (1): 768–76.

Chirila, E., and C. Draghici. 2011. "Analytical Approaches for Sampling and Sample Preparation for Heavy Metals Analysis in Biological Materials." In *Environmental Heavy Metal Pollution and Effects on Child Mental Development: Risk Assessment and Prevention Strategies,* edited by L. I. Simeonov, M. V. Kochubovski, and B. G. Simeonova, 129–43. Dordrecht, The Netherlands: Springer.

Cornelis, R., B. Heinzow, R. F. Herber, J. M. Christensen, O. M. Poulsen, E. Sabbioni, D. M. Templeton, Y. Thomassen, M. Vahter, and O. Vesterberg. 1995. "Sample Collection Guidelines for Trace Elements in Blood and Urine (Technical Report)." *Pure and Applied Chemistry* 67 (8–9): 1575–608.

Cornelis, R., B. Heinzow, R. F. Herber, J. M. Christensen, O. M. Poulsen, E. Sabbioni, D. M. Templeton, Y. Thomassen, M. Vahter, and O. Vesterberg. 1996. "Sample Collection Guidelines for Trace Elements in Blood and Urine." *Journal of Trace Elements in Medicine and Biology* 10 (2): 103–27.

Griffin, R. M. 1986. "Biological Monitoring for Heavy Metals: Practical Concerns." *Journal of Occupational and Environmental Medicine* 28 (8): 615–58.

Ianni, C., A. Bignasca, N. Calace, P. Rivaro, and E. Magi. "Bioaccessibility of Metals in Soils: Comparison between Chemical Extractions and *In Vitro* Tests." 2014. *Chemistry and Ecology* 30 (6): 541–54.

Ibanez, Y., B. Le Bot, and P. Glorennec. 2010. "House-Dust Metal Content and Bioaccessibility: A Review." *European Journal of Mineralogy* 22 (5): 629–37.

Jobanputra, N. K., R. Jones, G. Buckler, R. P. Cody, M. Gochfeld, T. M. Matte, D. Q. Rich, and G. G. Rhoads. 1998. "Accuracy and Reproducibility of Blood Lead Testing in Commercial Laboratories." *Archives of Pediatrics & Adolescent Medicine* 152 (6): 548–53.

Juhasz, A. L., E. Smith, C. Nelson, D. J. Thomas, and K. Bradham. 2014. "Variability Associated with As *In Vivo–In Vitro* Correlations When Using Different Bioaccessibility Methodologies." *Environmental Science & Technology* 48 (19): 11646–53.

Kummrow, F., F. F. Silva, R. Kuno, A. L. Souza, and P. V. Oliveira. 2008. "Biomonitoring Method for the Simultaneous Determination of Cadmium and Lead in Whole Blood by Electrothermal Atomic Absorption Spectrometry for Assessment of Environmental Exposure." *Talanta* 75 (1): 246–52.

Le Bot, B., J.-P. Lucas, F. Lacroix, and P. Glorennec. 2016. "Exposure of Children to Metals via Tap Water Ingestion at Home: Contamination and Exposure Data from a Nationwide Survey in France." *Environment International* 94: 500–507.

Li, J., K. Li, X.-Y. Cui, N. T. Basta, L.-P. Li, H.-B. Li, and L. Q. Ma. 2015. "*In Vitro* Bioaccessibility and *In Vivo* Relative Bioavailability in 12 Contaminated Soils: Method Comparison and Method Development." *Science of the Total Environment* 532: 812–20.

Ljung, K., A. Oomen, M. Duits, O. Selinus, and M. Berglund. 2007. "Bioaccessibility of Metals in Urban Playground Soils." *Journal of Environmental Science and Health Part A* 42 (9): 1241–50.

Oomen, A. G., A. Hack, M. Minekus, E. Zeijdner, C. Cornelis, G. Schoeters, W. Verstraete, Tom Van de Wiele, Joanna Wragg, Cathy J. M. Rompelberg, Adriënne J. A. M. Sips, and Joop H. Van Wijnen. 2002. "Comparison of Five *In Vitro* Digestion Models to Study the Bioaccessibility of Soil Contaminants." *Environmental Science & Technology* 36 (15): 3326–34.

Oomen, A. G., C. J. Rompelberg, M. A. Bruil, C. J. Dobbe, D. P. Pereboom, and A. J. Sips. 2003. "Development of an *In Vitro* Digestion Model for Estimating the Bioaccessibility of Soil Contaminants." *Archives of Environmental Contamination and Toxicology* 44 (3): 281–87.

Peijnenburg, W. J., M. Zablotskaja, and M. G. Vijver. 2007. "Monitoring Metals in Terrestrial Environments within a Bioavailability Framework and a Focus on Soil Extraction." *Ecotoxicology and Environmental Safety* 67 (2): 163–79.

Sheppard, B. S., D. T. Heitkemper, and C. M. Gaston. 1994. "Microwave Digestion for the Determination of Arsenic, Cadmium and Lead in Seafood Products by Inductively Coupled Plasma Atomic Emission and Mass Spectrometry." *Analyst* 119 (8): 1683–86.

Turner, A., and K. H. Ip. 2007. "Bioaccessibility of Metals in Dust from the Indoor Environment: Application of a Physiologically Based Extraction Test." *Environmental Science & Technology* 41 (22): 7851–56.

Sampling design

EPA (US Environmental Protection Agency). 2002. "Guidance on Choosing a Sampling Design for Environmental Data Collection for Use in Developing a Quality Assurance Plan." Guidance document, EPA, Washington, DC. https://www.epa.gov/sites/production/files/2015-06/documents/g5s-final.pdf.

Systematic grid sampling versus stratified random sampling

Gilbert, R. O., and B. A. Pulsipher. 2005. "Role of Sampling Designs in Obtaining Representative Data." *Environmental Forensics* 6 (1): 27–33.

Mattuck, R., R. Blanchet, and A. D. Wait. 2005. "Data Representativeness for Risk Assessment." *Environmental Forensics* 6 (1): 65–70.

PNNL (Pacific Northwest National Laboratory). n.d. "Visual Sample Plan." Software tool, PNNL, Richland, WA. https://vsp.pnnl.gov/.

Ramsey, C. A., and A. D. Hewitt. 2005. "A Methodology for Assessing Sample Representativeness." *Environmental Forensics* 6 (1): 71–75.

Zhu, A. X., J. Liu, F. Du, S. J. Zhang, C. Z. Qin, J. Burt, T. Behrens, and T. Scholten. 2015. "Predictive Soil Mapping with Limited Sample Data." *European Journal of Soil Science* 66 (3): 535–47.